D0773954

Romantic Cakes

PEGGY PORSCHEN

COOKIES AND CAKES TO CELEBRATE LOVE

Romantic Cakes

PEGGY PORSCHEN

PHOTOGRAPHY BY GEORGIA GLYNN SMITH

Quadrille

For Bryn with love

First published in 2007 by
Quadrille Publishing Limited,
Alhambra House, 27-31 Charing Cross Road,
London WC2H OLS

This paperback edition first published in 2008
Reprinted in 2009, 2010
10 9 8 7 6 5 4 3

Editorial Director: Jane O'Shea
Creative Director: Helen Lewis
Editor and Project Manager: Lewis Esson
Art Director: Chalkley Calderwood
Photography: Georgia Glynn Smith
Production: Ruth Deary

Text and designs © Peggy Porschen 2007
Photographs © Georgia Glynn Smith 2007
Edited text, design & layout © Quadrille Publishing Ltd 2007

The rights of Peggy Porschen to be identified as the Author of
this Work have been asserted by her in accordance with the
Copyright, Design and Patents Act 1988.

All rights reserved. No part of this book may be reproduced,
stored in a retrieval system or transmitted in any form or by any
means, electronic, electrostatic, magnetic tape, mechanical,
photocopying, recording or otherwise, without the prior permission
in writing of the publisher.

Cataloguing in Publication Data: a catalogue record for this book
is available from the British Library

ISBN 978-184400-629-8

Printed and bound in China.

Contents

Cookies

Luscious Lips

These cookie kisses make an ideal Valentine's Day gift. The bolder the colours, the better – here I used vibrant reds and pinks, with a sprinkle of edible glitter.

FOR ABOUT 20 COOKIES

about 400g royal icing (see page 136)

pink and red food colours

10–12 gingerbread cookies in the shape of lips, about 6x10 cm (2½ x 4 inches), made using 1 recipe quantity of gingerbread cookie dough (see page 119)

Disco Magenta sparkling glitter (EdAble Art)

Disco Red sparkling glitter (EdAble Art)

EQUIPMENT

2 SMALL BOWLS

SMALL PALETTE KNIFE

PAPER PIPING BAGS (SEE PAGE 137)

PAIR OF SCISSORS

CLING FILM OR DAMP CLOTH

SOFT BRUSH

1 Divide the royal icing equally between 2 bowls. Mix one amount of icing with pink food colour, the other with red. Add a little water until the icing has reached soft-peak consistency (see page 137). Fill one piping bag with each colour.

2 Snip a small tip off each piping bag and pipe around the sides of the lips in a steady smooth line (see 1 and page 138). Outline red lips with the red icing and pink lips with the pink icing. Cover the piping bags with cling film or a damp cloth to prevent the icing drying.

3 Dilute the remaining pink and red icing with a few drops of water to give each a runny consistency (see page 137). Fill one piping bag of each colour and flood the centres of the cookies (see 2), being careful not to overflow at the sides. For those with glitter, sprinkle a light dusting in the appropriate colour over the wet icing. Let dry.

4 Once dry, brush the excess glitter off the cookies where required and then pipe the detail on each cookie (see 3), using the reserved soft-peak icing. To enhance the lip shape, pipe the detail for the red lips with pink icing and the detail for the pink lips with red icing. Let dry.

Butterflies Away

I originally developed the idea for this table centrepiece with Vanessa Gore for a feature in *You & Your Wedding* magazine. You can find beautiful antique-style birdcages at markets or selected shops, but they are also available for hire. For a butterfly-themed wedding reception, combine these centrepieces with my Butterfly Miniature Wedding Cakes on pages 44–5.

FOR 15 COOKIES

15 cookies in 3 different shapes and sizes of butterfly, made using 1 recipe quantity of sugar cookie dough (see page 118)
about 600g royal icing (see page 136)

EQUIPMENT

SMALL ROUND CUTTER
SMALL BOWL
SMALL PALETTE KNIFE
PAPER PIPING BAGS (SEE PAGE 137)
PAIR OF SCISSORS
CLING FILM OR DAMP CLOTH
0.75M WHITE RIBBON

1 As soon as the cookies come out of the oven, cut a little hole at the top of one wing on each, using the small round cutter. Let them cool down.

2 Once the cookies are cold, start by mixing the icing with a little water until it has reached soft-peak consistency (see page 137). Put some of the icing into a piping bag.

3 Snip a small tip off the bag and pipe the outlines of the wings (see page 138). Keep the bag with the leftover icing covered with cling film or damp cloth to prevent the icing drying out.

4 Dilute the remaining icing with a few drops of water to a runny consistency (see page 137). Put into a fresh piping bag. Again, snip the tip off the bag and fill the centre of the wings with the runny icing, being careful not to overflow the sides. Let dry.

5 Once they are dry, pipe the body and the detail, i.e. swirls and small dots, on to the wings, using the soft-peak icing. Let dry.

6 Once they are completely dry (ideally leave overnight), push a piece of ribbon through each hole and carefully hang them up inside and outside the birdcage.

Bride and Groom Cookies

Use these as wedding favours or as a token to accompany your gift.
To add a personal touch, match the designs to the real wedding gowns.

FOR 3 BRIDE AND 3 GROOM COOKIES

about 600g royal icing (see page 136)

black food colour

3 cookies made in the shape of prom dresses
(about 12.5x10cm/5x4 inches) and 3 in the
shape of tuxedos (about 7.5x11cm/
3x4½inches) made using 1 recipe quantity
of sugar cookie dough (see page 118)

EQUIPMENT

2 SMALL BOWLS

SMALL PALETTE KNIFE

PAPER PIPING BAGS (SEE PAGE 137)

PAIR OF SCISSORS

CLING FILM OR A DAMP CLOTH

1 Divide the icing between two bowls, about 250g in one and 350g in the other.
Mix the 250g with black food colour. Add a little water to both bowls until the icings
have reached soft-peak consistency (see page 137). Fill one piping bag with each colour.

2 Snip a small tip off the bag with black icing and pipe the outline of each groom in
a steady smooth line (see 1 and page 138). Do the same with the white icing on the bride
cookies. Cover the bags with cling film or damp cloth to prevent the icing drying out.

3 Dilute the remaining white and black icing with a few drops of water to a runny
consistency (see page 137). Fill one piping bag with each colour and flood the centres of
the cookies in the appropriate colours, being careful not to overflow the sides. Flood the
tuxedo centres with white first (see 2), let dry and then flood the black part (see 3).

4 Once dry, pipe the detail on each cookie, using the soft-peak icing (see 4). Let dry.

Heart-shaped Place Cards

This clever idea turns a simple heart cookie into a stunning decorative feature at the dinner table of a wedding or engagement party. You can use other cookie shapes as well, as long as they provide enough space for writing names on the top. If you find using the ribbon too fiddly, you can wrap each heart in a cellophane bag and place it on top of each dinner plate. This way your guests can take the cookie home as a personalized keepsake.

FOR 10 COOKIES

10 cookies made in heart shapes (about 6cm/2½ inches) using ½ recipe quantity of sugar cookie dough (see page 118)
350g royal icing (see page 136)
dusky-pink and dark-brown food colours (Sugarflair)

EQUIPMENT

SMALL ROUND CUTTER
SMALL BOWL
SMALL PALETTE KNIFE
PAPER PIPING BAGS (SEE PAGE 137)
PAIR OF SCISSORS
CLING FILM OR DAMP CLOTH
1.25M PASTEL-PINK RIBBON, 15 MM WIDTH

1 As soon as the heart cookies come out of the oven, cut a little hole at the top of each, using the small round cutter. Be careful as the tray will be hot. Let them cool down.

2 Once the cookies are cold, start with the brown outline. In a bowl, mix about 300g icing with a small amount of brown colour. Add a little water until it has reached soft-peak consistency (see page 137). Put some of the icing into a piping bag. Snip a small tip off the piping bag and pipe around the outlines of the hearts (see page 138).

3 Should you have any icing left over in the bag, squeeze it back into the bowl with the remaining brown icing and dilute it with a few drops of water to a runny consistency (see page 137). Put this into a fresh piping bag. Again, snip the tip off and fill the centre of the cookies with the runny icing, being careful not to overflow the sides. Let dry.

4 Once dry, mix the remaining royal icing with dusky-pink food colour and a little water to soft-peak consistency. Put it into a piping bag, snip off a small tip and pipe a squiggly outline around the sides of the hearts. Pipe names or initials in the centre. Let dry.

5 Once completely dry (ideally leave overnight), push a piece of ribbon through the hole and tie into a knot or a bow. Attach to a champagne glass or a napkin as a place card.

Rosebud Cookies

To complement the rosebud design, I have scented the icing with rosewater. Wrapped in a pretty gift box or cellophane bags, these gorgeous little cookies make an exquisite gift or wedding favour.

FOR ABOUT 10 COOKIES

about 450g royal icing (see page 136)

red, pink and green food colours

small amount of rosewater

12 cookies in the shape of rosebuds, made from 1 recipe quantity of vanilla sugar cookie dough (see page 118)

EQUIPMENT

SEVERAL SMALL BOWLS

SMALL PALETTE KNIFE

FEW PAPER PIPING BAGS (SEE PAGE 137)

PAIR OF SCISSORS

CLING FILM OR A DAMP CLOTH

1 Place about 300g of royal icing in a bowl and colour it with red food colour. Add a few drops of rosewater until the icing has reached soft-peak consistency (see page 137). Put a small amount in a piping bag.

2 Snip a small tip off the piping bag and pipe the outlines for the flowering top of the buds on the cookies, leaving enough space for the green leaves at the bottom of the cookies. Pipe all the red outlines first.

3 Should you have any red icing left over in the bag, squeeze it back into the bowl with the remaining red icing and dilute it with a few drops of rosewater to a runny consistency (see page 137). Put this in a fresh piping bag. Again, snip a tip off the piping bag and fill the red-outline centres of the bud heads with the runny icing, being careful not to overflow the sides. Let dry before piping on the green stems.

4 Once the red icing has dried completely, take about 100g of icing and colour it green. Put a small amount in a piping bag, pipe the outline of the stems first, then, as in step 3, make some runny green icing and flood the centres with that and fill the centres of the stems. Let dry. Reserve a small amount of soft-peak green icing to trace the outline of the stems and leaves later.

5 Mix the remaining 50g of icing with pink food colour and trace the individual petals of the rose buds. Let dry.

6 Once dry, trace the outline of the stems using the reserved green icing. Let dry.

Wedding Cake Cookies

This idea gives you the option of coordinating the design of your wedding favour with your wedding cake, making a lovely memento for your guests to take home or to send to those who were unable to make it – if they live overseas, for example.

FOR 6 COOKIES

600g royal icing (see page 136)

baby-blue food colour

6 cookies in the shape of wedding cakes (about 10x12.5cm/4x5 inches), made using 1 recipe quantity of sugar cookie dough, see page 118)

EQUIPMENT

SMALL BOWL

SMALL PALETTE KNIFE

PAPER PIPING BAGS (SEE PAGE 137)

PAIR OF SCISSORS

CLING FILM OR DAMP CLOTH

1 In a small bowl, mix about 450g of royal icing with a little water to soft-peak consistency (see page 137). Put some of the icing into a piping bag.

2 Snip a small tip off the piping bag and pipe the outline of the cake shape for each cookie in a steady smooth line (see page 138). Cover the piping bag with the leftover icing with cling film or a damp cloth to prevent it drying out.

3 Dilute the remaining icing with a few drops of water to a runny consistency (see page 137). Put it in a piping bag and flood the centres of the cookies, being careful not to overflow the sides. Let dry.

4 Once dry, mix 150g of icing with a little blue food colour and a small amount of water to give a soft-peak consistency (see page 137). Pipe the outline of the bow detail on each cookie. Cover the piping bag with any leftover icing with cling film or a damp cloth to prevent it drying out.

5 Dilute the remaining blue icing with a small amount of water to a runny consistency (see page 137), put it in a piping bag and use to flood the centre of the bow. Let dry.

6 With the remaining soft-peak white icing, pipe the outline for the individual cake tiers and a dotted border at the bottom. With the remaining soft-peak blue icing, pipe the detail of the bow. Let dry.

Risqué Lingerie

Make little goodie bags filled with these lingerie cookies
for friends at your hen night. If you are already married, make them for your
husband to give him a taste of what is in store for later.

FOR ABOUT 4 **ONE-PIECE LINGERIE
COOKIES AND** 4 **TWO-PIECE COOKIES**

600g royal icing (see page 136)

pink and red food colours

4 cookies in the shape of a one-piece swim
suit (about 6x10cm/2½x4 inches) and
4 cookies each in the shape of bras and
knickers (about 7.5cm/3 inch square),
made using 1 recipe quantity of sugar or
gingerbread cookie dough (see pages 118–19)

EQUIPMENT

3 SMALL BOWLS

SMALL PALETTE KNIFE

PAPER PIPING BAGS (SEE PAGE 137)

PAIR OF SCISSORS

CLING FILM OR A DAMP CLOTH

1 Divide the royal icing equally between 3 small bowls. Colour one with pink and one
with red food colour, and keep the third one white. Add a small amount of water to each
until the icing has reached soft-peak consistency (see page 137). Put a small amount of
each colour into a piping bag and keep the remaining icing covered with cling film or a
damp cloth to prevent it drying out.

2 Snip a small tip off each bag and pipe the outlines for the bras, the knickers and
the camisoles for each cookie (see 1). Keep the piping bags covered with cling film to
prevent the icing from drying out.

3 Dilute the icing remaining in the bowls with a small amount of water to a runny
consistency (see page 137) and put into 3 fresh piping bags. Flood the centres of each
cookie with the same colour as the outline, then use a different colour to pipe little dots
on the still-wet base (see 2). This way the dots will sink in and form a smooth surface
with the main icing. Let dry.

4 Once everything is dry,
pipe the details, i.e. the frills,
straps and little bows, using
the reserved soft-peak icing
(see 3). Let dry.

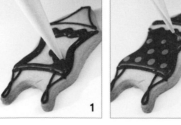

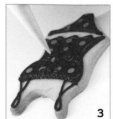

Celestial Lovers

The twinkling stars and golden moon have inspired lovers since the beginning of time. There is more than a hint of night-sky magic about these little cookies.

FOR 5 CRESCENT MOONS AND 15 STAR COOKIES

about 400g royal icing (see page 136)

black food colour

5 cookies in the shape of crescent moons (about 5x10cm/2x4inches) and 15 in the shape of small stars (about 3.5cm/ 1½inches), made using 1 recipe quantity of sugar cookie dough (see page 118)

Hologram Silver Glitter Sparkle (EdAble Art)

EQUIPMENT

SMALL BOWL

SMALL PALETTE KNIFE

PAPER PIPING BAGS (SEE PAGE 137)

PAIR OF SCISSORS

SOFT BRUSH

CLING FILM OR DAMP CLOTH

1 Place the royal icing in a bowl and mix it with a small amount of black food colour to a light grey shade. Add a little water until the icing has reached soft-peak consistency (see page 137). Put some of the icing into a piping bag. Keep the remaining icing covered with cling film or a damp cloth to prevent it drying out.

2 Snip a small tip off the piping bag and pipe the outlines of the moon and the stars in a steady smooth line (see page 138).

3 Dilute the remaining icing with a few drops of water to a runny consistency (see page 137). Fill a fresh piping bag with this.

4 Again snip off the tip and fill the centre of the cookies with the runny icing, being careful not to overflow the sides.

5 While the icing is still wet, drizzle a small amount of glitter over the cookies and then let dry.

6 Once the icing is dry, carefully use the soft brush to dust the excess glitter off the cookies.

Carnival in Venice

I made these as wedding favours for my mother-in-law to be, Georgina Harvey, and her new husband, Rog, and dedicate this design to them. Their wedding theme was Venetian, and the white mask is an almost exact copy of the one the bride wore. All their guests got masks too, so I added sticks to the white ones for the ladies, and ribbons to the men's golden masks to tie them round their heads.

FOR 10 COOKIES

1 recipe quantity of gingerbread cookie dough (see page 119)

600g royal icing (see page 136)

ivory food colour (Wilton)

Gold Hologram Glitter Sparkle (EdAble Art)

Gold Lustre (Sugar Flair)

small amount of clear alcohol

small amount of sugar flower paste (Squires Kitchen)

small amount of icing sugar

EQUIPMENT

SMALL NON-STICK PLASTIC BOARD

SMALL ROLLING PIN

5 COOKIE STICKS (WILTON)

MASK AND EYE CUTTERS

SMALL KITCHEN KNIFE

BAKING TRAY

WIRE RACK

2 SMALL BOWLS

SMALL PALETTE KNIFE

CLING FILM OR DAMP CLOTH

PAPER PIPING BAGS (SEE PAGE 137)

PAIR OF SCISSORS

SOFT BRUSH FOR DUSTING

FINE ARTIST'S BRUSH

5 M THIN GOLD RIBBON

2 FLOWER CUTTERS (1 LARGE, 1 SMALL)

COLOUR MIXING PALETTE

2.5 M IVORY AND GOLD RIBBON

1 On a non-stick plastic board, roll out half the cookie dough until about 1cm thick. Place about one-third of a cookie stick underneath the dough and keep rolling the dough over the stick until the dough is just about 1mm thicker than the stick.

2 Place the mask cutter over the top, with the cookie stick to one side. Push down and cut around the cutter with a small knife where necessary. Use the separate eye-shaped cutter to cut out eye holes. Carefully transfer to a baking tray. Repeat until you have 5 masks on sticks. Repeat the rolling and cutting without sticks to make 5 more masks.

3 Bake as described on page 119 and leave to cool on a wire rack.

TO MAKE THE GOLDEN MASKS

4 Place 300g of royal icing in a small bowl. Mix in enough ivory food colour to produce a strong ivory colour Add a few drops of water and mix to a soft peak consistency (see page 137). Put some of the icing into a piping bag. Keep the remaining icing covered.

5 Snip a small tip off the bag and pipe the outline of the gold masks in a smooth steady line (see page 138). Cover the bag with cling film or a damp cloth to prevent it drying out.

6 Add a little more water to the remaining icing to produce a runny consistency (see page 137). Put it into a fresh piping bag and use to flood the cookie centres.

7 While the icing is still wet, sprinkle a light dusting of gold glitter over the top and then let dry completely. Once the icing on the cookies is dry, brush off the excess glitter.

8 Use the bag of soft-peak ivory icing to pipe a swirl design around the eyes. Let dry.

9 Once the swirls are dry, mix a small amount of gold lustre with a drop of alcohol to a thick paste. Use a fine artist's brush to paint the swirls with the gold. Let dry overnight.

10 Once dry, tie a piece of gold ribbon through the holes for the eyes on each side.

TO MAKE THE IVORY MASKS

11 Place the remaining icing in another small bowl and colour to a pale ivory. Add a few drops of water and mix to a soft-peak consistency. Put some into a piping bag. Keep the remaining icing covered.

12 Repeat steps 5 and 6, using the pale ivory icing.

13 Make the sugar flowers. Roll the sugar paste out on the plastic board dusted with icing sugar until very thin. Cut out a selection of little sugar flowers.

14 Place each flower into a well of the colour-mixing palette to let them dry. This way they will dry in a rounded/curved shape.

15 Once the icing is dry, stick the little flowers on top using a small dab of icing.

16 Using a piping bag filled with ivory soft-peak royal icing, pipe the swirls and dots around the eyes and the flower centres. Let dry overnight.

17 Finish the cookies by tying a bow of ribbon around the top of each cookie stick.

Mini Heart Favours

For obvious reasons, iced heart-shaped cookies are among the most popular choices for wedding favours. What makes this particular version so pretty is wrapping the three different shades of pink together in a bag. This idea works for any colour scheme. Instead of using them as favours, you can serve them individually as petits fours, arranged on a cake stand or at the side of a coffee cup.

FOR 24 COOKIES

about 300g royal icing (see page 136)

pink food colour

24 cookies in small heart shapes (about 3.5cm/1½inch), made using ½ recipe quantity of sugar cookie dough (see page 118)

EQUIPMENT

SMALL BOWL

SMALL PALETTE KNIFE

PAPER PIPING BAGS (SEE PAGE 137)

PAIR OF SCISSORS

CLING FILM OR DAMP CLOTH

8 CELLOPHANE BAGS (OPTIONAL)

ABOUT 4 M PINK SATIN RIBBON (OPTIONAL)

1 Start with the lightest shade of pink. In a bowl, mix one-third of the royal icing with a tiny drop of pink food colour to give a pastel-pink shade. Add a little water until the icing is soft-peak consistency (see page 137). Put some of the icing into a piping bag. Keep the bowl covered.

2 Snip a small tip off the piping bag and pipe the outline of the heart in a steady smooth line (see page 138). Outline 8 of the hearts with the pastel-pink icing.

3 Should you have any icing left over in the bag, squeeze it back into the bowl with the remaining pastel-pink icing and dilute it with a few drops of water to a runny consistency (see page 137). Fill a fresh piping bag with this.

4 Again snip off the tip and fill the centre of the hearts with the runny icing, being careful not to overflow the sides.

5 Repeat steps 1 to 4, using 2 darker shades of pink icing, so you have 8 cookies in each shade.

6 If you like, you can pack 1 of each shade of cookie in a cellophane bag and tie this up decoratively with ribbon.

Tea for Two

These funky retro-inspired teapots and teacups make the perfect
addition to a vintage-style bridal tea party.

FOR 4 **TEAPOT AND** 4 **TEACUP COOKIES**

about 600g royal icing (see page 136)

pink, blue and green food colours

4 cookies in the shape of teapots (about
7.5x10cm/3x4 inch) and 4 in the shape of
teacups (about 7.5x8.5cm/3x3½inches),
made using 1 recipe quantity of sugar
cookie dough (see page 118)

EQUIPMENT

3 SMALL BOWLS

SMALL PALETTE KNIFE

PAPER PIPING BAGS (SEE PAGE 137)

PAIR OF SCISSORS

CLING FILM OR A DAMP CLOTH

1 Divide the royal icing equally between 3 bowls. Mix one amount of icing with pink
and one with blue food colour, and keep the other one white. Add a little water to all
three until they have reached soft-peak consistency (see page 137). Fill one piping bag
with each colour.

2 One at a time, snip a small tip off each piping bag and pipe the outline of each cookie
in a steady smooth line (see page 138), decorating one cup and one teapot in each colour.
Cover the piping bags with cling film or a damp cloth to prevent the icing drying out.

3 Dilute each of the remaining bowls of icing with a few drops of water to a runny
consistency (see page 137). Fill one piping bag with each colour and flood the centres of
the appropriately coloured cookies, being careful not to overflow the sides.

4 Once they are dry, pipe the outlines, including the lids and handles, using a contrast-
ing colour (white on pink or blue on white), using the soft-peak icing.

5 Using the soft-peak icing, pipe different designs on each cookie, such as polka dots,
stripes, hearts and little rosebuds. For the little leaves of the rosebuds, mix some leftover
white icing with green food colour, snip the tip of the piping bag in a V shape and pipe
the leaves. Let dry.

Heart-shaped Sugar Cubes

Although this doesn't involve baking, I couldn't resist adding this simple but very sweet idea to my romantic portfolio. You can use any shape you like.

FOR ABOUT 12 SUGAR CUBES

about 6 tablespoons granulated sugar
pink, blue and yellow food colours

EQUIPMENT

SMALL BOWLS
GREASEPROOF PAPER
SMALL HEART-SHAPED COOKIE CUTTER
TEASPOON

1 Divide the sugar equally between 3 small bowls, then add a tiny drop of each food colour and a little water to each to make it damp. Mix until evenly coloured.

2 On a piece of greaseproof paper, push a small amount of sugar firmly into the heart cutter (see 1) and level the top with a spoon (see 2). Carefully lift off the cutter and let dry (see 3 and 4).

3 Repeat until all the sugar in each colour is used up.

Mini Cakes

JE T'AIME MON AMOUR 36 ♦ CHOCOLATE BOW CANDY CAKES 38

FORGET-ME-NOT FANCIES 42 ♦ BUTTERFLY MINIATURE WEDDING CAKES 44

RIBBON ROSE CUP CAKES 48 ♦ CHOCOLATE HEARTS 52 ♦ ROCOCO CUP CAKES 56

WHITE SPRING POSIES 60 ♦ TIFFANY-STYLE SUGAR BOXES 64

SPRING BLOSSOM CUP CAKES 68

Je T'aime Mon Amour...

This simple presentation of little alphabet cakes makes a uniquely personal gift. You can ice any message in this way, or even make it more intriguing by arranging the letters randomly as a kind of puzzle, letting the recipient put the message together.

FOR A MESSAGE LIKE THIS ONE, OF ABOUT 15 LETTERS

about 15 fondant fancies made as described on pages 133–4, using a 15cm (6-inch) square Victoria sponge (½ recipe quantity, see the guide on page 143) and red fondant icing

about 250g royal icing

pink and red food colours

EQUIPMENT

ABOUT 15 ROUND SILVER METALLIC MUFFIN CASES (THEY DON'T MAKE SQUARE ONES, BUT THESE MOULD TO SHAPE)

SMALL BOWL

SMALL PALETTE KNIFE

PAPER PIPING BAGS (SEE PAGE 137)

PAIR OF SCISSORS

GIFT BOX, WRAPPING PAPER AND RIBBON (OPTIONAL)

1 Place the fondant fancies into the silver muffin cases. Only round muffin cases are usually available, so you need to shape them round the fondant fancies (see page 134).

2 Place about 200g of royal icing in a small bowl. Using a small palette knife, mix it with pink food colour and a few drops of water until at soft-peak consistency (see page 137). Fill some of the icing into a piping bag and keep the remainder in the covered bowl.

3 Snip the tip off a piping bag and pipe the outlines of the letters on the fondant fancies.

4 If you have any icing left inside the bag, squeeze it back into the bowl and dilute the icing with water, this time to a runny consistency (see page 137). Put this in a new piping bag and use to flood the letter centres. Be careful not to let it overflow the sides.

5 Mix the remaining 50g of icing with red food colour and enough water to achieve a slight runny consistency. Put it in a fresh piping bag, snip off a small tip and pipe little dots into the still-wet pink icing of the letters. Let dry.

6 Arrange the cakes to spell out your personal message (or jumble them), in a gift box if you like.

Chocolate Bow Candy Cakes

These cakes are ideal for a small wedding, as you can make a tiered
miniature wedding cake per guest instead of one large wedding cake.
As they travel well and look very pretty in a clear gift box,
they also make stunning wedding favours.

FOR ABOUT 6 MINI TIERED WEDDING CAKES

about 250g ready-made dark-brown
   chocolate-flavoured sugar paste
gum tragacanth
icing sugar for dusting
edible glue
six 7.5cm (3-inch) and six 3.5cm (1½-inch)
   round cakes, made from a 30cm (12-inch)
   square rich dark chocolate cake (see page
   124), flavoured and soaked to choice, then
   covered with marzipan and pastel-blue,
   green and yellow sugar paste (2 of each
   type of cake in each colour, see pages 125–8)
small amount of royal icing (see page 136)
dark-brown and willow-green (Wilton) food
   colours

EQUIPMENT

CLING FILM OR DAMP CLOTH
SMALL NON-STICK PLASTIC BOARD
SMALL ROLLING PIN
SMALL KITCHEN KNIFE
DESIGN WHEELER (PME)
SMALL BRUSH
KITCHEN PAPER
BOW CUTTER (JEM)

FOR THE BLUE CAKES

➧1 Mix the dark brown chocolate sugar paste with a little gum tragacanth. Wrap in cling
film and let rest for about half an hour until the paste is flexible.

➧2 On a plastic board dusted with icing sugar, roll out the paste and cut it into strips
15mm (⅜ inch) wide, then roll the design wheeler along the edges.

➧3 To make each bow, cut a strip 10cm (4 inches) long and turn upside down. Fold both ends
over and glue down in the middle, supporting the loops with kitchen paper. Cut another
strip about 3cm (1¼ inches) long, fold it over the joint and fix with edible glue. Let dry.

➧4 Cut 4 strips about 15cm (6 inches) in length and lay them down the sides of the cake,
fixing them with edible glue. Cut 4 thin strips to place in between the spaces at the bottom.

5 To finish each bow, cut 2 more pieces of brown paste about 4cm (1½ inches) long and snip the ends in a V shape. Stick on the top tier with edible glue, then the bow.

FOR THE GREEN CAKES

6 On a plastic board dusted with icing sugar, thinly roll out the brown paste. Cut out the shapes for the bows using the bow cutter. Assemble the bows as before. Let dry.

7 Divide the top tier of the green cake into 3 and the bottom tier into 5 even parts and mark them with small dots around the edge.

8 Roll out another piece of brown paste and cut out strips about 1cm (½ inch) wide and 4–6cm (1½–2½ inches) in length.

9 Twist each strip with your fingers and attach to the sides of the cake with edible glue.

10 Now stick the brown bows on top of the joins, using a small amount of chocolate-brown royal icing.

11 Mix a small amount of icing with green colour to soft-peak consistency (see page 137) and pipe small dots around the base of each tier.

FOR THE YELLOW CAKES

12 On a plastic board dusted with icing sugar, thinly roll out the brown paste. Cut out a 5mm (¼ inch) thin strip to go around the base of the bottom tier and a 2.5cm (1 inch) thick strip to go around the base of the top tier. Fix them both in place with edible glue.

13 To make the bow, cut out a 1.5cm (⅝-inch) wide and 10cm (4-inch) long strip from the paste, fold both ends over to the middle and glue them down, supporting the loops with kitchen paper. Cut another strip about 3cm (1¼ inches) in length, fold it over the join and fix it with some edible glue. Let dry.

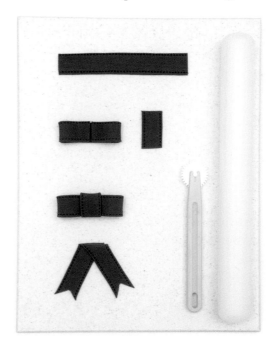

14 To finish the bow, cut 2 more pieces of brown paste of about 4cm (1½ inches) in length and snip the ends off in a V shape. Place them on the side of top tier with brown icing or edible glue and stick the bow on top.

Forget-Me-Not Fancies

These little delights make perfect cakes for a celebration tea or can be served as petits fours. The forget-me-not motif also makes them a great idea for a token to wish someone farewell – say, the bride and groom going on honeymoon.

FOR 16 FONDANT FANCIES

16 fondant fancies (made as described on pages 133–4) using a 15cm (6-inch) square Victoria sponge flavoured to your choice) and dipped in pastel-lilac fondant icing

about 100g white sugar flower paste

blue and yellow food colours

icing sugar or cornflour for dusting

small amount of royal icing (see page 136)

EQUIPMENT

16 METALLIC SILVER MUFFIN CASES

NON-STICK BOARD WITH HOLES (CEL BOARD)

SMALL ROLLING PIN

SMALL 5-PETAL FLOWER CUTTER

BONE TOOL

PETAL FLUTING/POINTED END TOOL (JEM)

STAYFRESH MULTI MAT

PAPER PIPING BAGS (SEE PAGE 137)

PAIR OF SCISSORS

1 Place the fondant fancies in silver paper cases as described on page 134.

2 Colour the sugar flower paste pastel blue by kneading in a small amount of the colour.

3 Lightly dust the plastic board with icing sugar and place a small piece of the paste over the medium-sized hole, then roll it out until very thin. Turn the paste upside down and place your flower cutter over the area of the raised knot and cut out the flower.

4 Carefully lift the flower and curve it around the bone tool to form a cup. Gently push the tip of the pointed tool into the centre of the flower. Let dry. Make about 48 in the same way.

5 Once the curved flowers are dry, stick a cluster of 'forget-me-nots' on to each fondant fancy using small dabs of royal icing.

6 Mix a small amount of royal icing with yellow food colour, put it in a piping bag, snip a small tip off the bag and pipe little yellow dots in the centre of the flowers.

7 Squeeze the remaining icing out off the bag, add a drop of blue colour and mix to a soft green. Put in a fresh bag, snip a V shape in the tip and pipe little leaves around the flowers.

Butterfly Miniature Wedding Cakes

The mix of butterflies in different sizes, some on their own and some in pairs, gives each individual cake interest to the eye. To create the look of a 'living swarm' of butterflies I have arranged some individual butterflies on the pillars and the tiers of the cake stand. As a symbol of love and union, a large butterfly couple decorates the top tier, which can be used as the cutting cake.

FOR ABOUT 25 MINIATURE CAKES AND 1 15CM (6-INCH) TOP TIER CAKE

small amount of white vegetable fat
about 350g royal icing
25 miniature cakes (5cm / 2-inch diameter) cut from a 30cm (12 inch) square of sponge cake and one 15cm (6-inch) round cake, made using 4½ recipe quantities of Victoria sponge mixture, trimmed, soaked and flavoured to choice, then covered with marzipan and a thin layer of white sugar paste as described on pages 127–31

EQUIPMENT

SHEETS OF CELLOPHANE
SMALL BOWL
SMALL PALETTE KNIFE
PAPER PIPING BAGS (SEE PAGE 137)
PAIR OF SCISSORS
CLING FILM OR A DAMP CLOTH
THIN CARDBOARD
GREASEPROOF PAPER
ABOUT 6 M WHITE SATIN RIBBON, 15 MM WIDTH

Make the butterflies at least 2 days in advance. You'll need 2 large butterflies for the top tier and about 20 medium and 20 small ones.

1 Place a sheet of cellophane on top of the butterfly template (see inside front cover) and rub it with a very thin layer of vegetable fat.

2 Mix the royal icing with a little water to soft-peak consistency (see page 137) and put some in a piping bag. Snip a small tip off the bag and pipe the outline for the wings on the cellophane. Keep the icing in the bowl covered with cling film or a damp cloth to prevent it drying out.

3 Dilute about 250g of the icing with a small amount of water to a runny consistency (see page 137). Fill a piping bag with it and flood the centres of the butterfly wing outlines. To avoid the icing of both wings running together, flood only one part first and let that set before you flood the other part. Let these butterflies dry completely overnight.

4 Once dry, decorate the wings with piped swirls and dots, using soft-peak royal icing. Let dry.

5 Take a piece of thin cardboard (I use the lid of a cake box) and fold it like an accordion (see page 80). Then cut a sheet of greaseproof paper into strips to line the cardboard folds.

6 Once the decorated wings are completely dry, carefully take them off the cellophane. Pipe the bodies for the butterflies into the folds of the greaseproof paper and stick the butterfly wings together as shown on page 80 . Let them dry for a couple of hours to ensure they stick together securely.

TO DECORATE THE CAKES

7 Cut the ribbon into pieces long enough to cover the sides of the cakes and arrange the pieces around the base of each cake, securing them with dabs of royal icing.

8 Pipe small dots along the edge of the ribbon, using soft-peak royal icing (see 1).

9 Once the butterflies are dry, stick them on top of the cakes with dabs of icing (see 2). Arrange a few butterfly pairs and a few single ones on top of the miniature cakes and finish the top tier with a large butterfly couple.

Ribbon Rose Cup Cakes

These feature a very pretty type of rose made using a simple
technique. As it looks like a piece of ribbon rolled together to form
a little rosebud, I have called it a 'ribbon rose'.

FOR 12 CUP CAKES

about 200g sugar paste

red, pink and green food colours

icing sugar for dusting

12 cup cakes, made using ½ recipe quantity
Victoria sponge (see page 122), flavoured
to choice, baked in silver metallic muffin
cases, soaked with syrup and iced with pink
and purple fondant icing (see pages 133–5)

small amount of royal icing (see page 136)

EQUIPMENT

CLING FILM

SMALL NON-STICK PLASTIC BOARD

SMALL ROLLING PIN

LEAF CUTTER

SMALL KITCHEN KNIFE

PAPER PIPING BAG (SEE PAGE 137)

PAIR OF SCISSORS

▸1 Mix about 75g of the sugar paste with red colour, 75g with pink and 50g with green.
Always keep paste you are not using covered with cling film to prevent it drying out.

▸2 On a plastic board lightly dusted with icing
sugar, roll a piece of pink or red sugar paste out
to about 3cm (1¼ inches) wide, 8cm (3¼ inches)
long and about 1mm (¹⁄₂₄ inch) thick. Trim the
edges and fold the strip over in half lengthwise
down its width, pinching it at intervals to get a
pleated effect, as shown. Now roll the folded
strip up from one side to the other and pinch off
the excess at the bottom of the flower shape.
Let dry. You'll need 6 pink and 6 red roses.

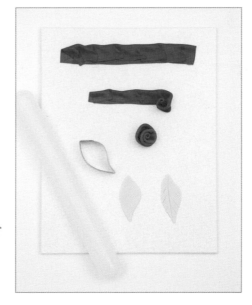

▸3 For the leaves, roll out a thin piece of green
sugar paste and cut out 24 leaves using the leaf
cutter. Mark the leaf veins down the middle
using a small kitchen knife. Shape the leaves
slightly with your fingers and let dry.

▸4 Once the roses and leaves are dry, stick them on top of the cup cakes using a dab of
royal icing to fix them in place.

Chocolate Hearts

These little French-style chocolate heart cakes make a delightful alternative to chocolate or chocolate truffles. I used an old-fashioned crimping technique for the border design on the monogram heart, which gives this classic design a touch of 'retro revival'.

FOR 24 SMALL CAKES

24 small cakes made using 1½ recipe quantities of rich dark chocolate sponge (see page 124), baked in miniature heart-shaped baking tins (about 5cm/2 inches across)

2 tablespoon sieved apricot jam

icing sugar for dusting

about 1kg dark-brown chocolate-flavoured sugar paste

a little edible glue or alcohol

small amount of royal icing (see page 136)

pink food colour

about 200g white sugar paste

pink edible lustre

EQUIPMENT

SMALL KITCHEN KNIFE

SMALL SAUCEPAN

PASTRY BRUSH

ROLLING PIN

5MM (1/4-INCH) MARZIPAN SPACERS

SERRATED CRIMPING TOOL

SMALL ROLLING PIN WITH A LINED SURFACE

PAPER PIPING BAGS (SEE PAGE 137)

PAIR OF SCISSORS

SMALL HEART CUTTER

FINE ARTIST'S BRUSH

1 Level the top of the heart sponges by trimming off the top crust with a kitchen knife. Gently heat up the apricot jam and thinly brush it all over the little sponges.

2 On a smooth surface dusted with icing sugar, roll out the chocolate sugar paste between the marzipan spacers to a piece large enough to cover the top and sides of the cakes. Lay it over them and carefully push it down the sides. Trim the excess paste off using a kitchen knife.

FOR THE MONOGRAM HEART CAKES

3 Roll a small amount of chocolate paste to a sausage long enough to cover the circumference of the heart. Brush the base of each cake thinly with edible glue or alcohol and lay the sausage around the sides.

4 Gently push the crimper all around the base, creating a continuous patterned border.

5 Mix a small amount of royal icing with pink food colour and a bit of water to produce soft-peak consistency (see page 137) and put it into a piping bag. Pipe the monogram on top of each cake.

FOR THE DOTTED HEART CAKES

6 Mix the white sugar paste with a small amount of pink food colour and roll it out on the plastic board dusted with icing sugar to a strip long enough to cover the base of each heart. Roll once over that with the lined rolling pin to give it a lined pattern, then cut it into a long strip about 1cm (½ inch) wide.

7 Brush a thin strip around the base of each cake with edible glue and lay the pink strip around it.

8 Pipe little dots of pink royal icing all over the top of the cakes. Let dry.

FOR THE HEARTS ON HEART CAKES

9 On a plastic board dusted lightly with icing sugar, roll out some pink sugar paste until very thin. Using the heart cutter, cut out little heart shapes and dust them with pink lustre.

10 Brush the back of each heart thinly with edible glue and randomly arrange the pink hearts all over the cakes. Let dry.

Rococo Cup Cakes

A lot of my designs are inspired by fashion and jewellery.
The inspiration for these cup cakes comes from a photograph I saw in a bridal
magazine of a beautiful French antique-style looped earring studded with
little lilac blossoms and draped jewels, worn by a model in a frilled eau-de-Nil
dress. The whole effect is very Marie Antoinette. I love the colour
combination of green, lilac and gold. Let them eat cake...

FOR 12 CUP CAKES

about 150g sugar flower paste

purple and green food colours

icing sugar or cornflour, for dusting

small amount of royal icing

12 cup cakes (flavoured to your choice),
    made from ½ recipe quantity of
    Victoria sponge baked in gold cup cake
    cases, soaked with syrup and iced with
    eau-de-Nil coloured fondant icing, as
    described on pages 133–5

pink or silver sparkling sugar pearls

EQUIPMENT

SMALL BOWLS

SMALL PLASTIC BOARD

SMALL ROLLING PIN

CLING FILM

PETUNIA FLOWER CUTTER

FOAM PAD

BONE TOOL

FLOWER VEINER

SMALL PAINTER'S PALETTE

SMALL CALYX CUTTER

PAPER PIPING BAGS (SEE PAGE 137)

PAIR OF SCISSORS

1 Mix the flower paste with the purple food colour to produce a soft lilac shade.

2 On the plastic board lightly dusted with icing sugar or cornflour, roll some of this lilac paste out very thinly. Cover the rest with cling film to prevent it drying out.

3 Using the petunia cutter, cut out 12 large flower shapes, place them on top of the foam pad and smooth the edges using the bone tool. Press the flower veiner gently on top of each flower and place it into a well of a painter's palette to let it dry in a curved shape.

4 Roll out the remaining paste and, using a small calyx cutter, cut out about 120 small flowers. Slightly curve them between your fingers and let them dry. (You will need about 10 small flowers per cup cake.)

5 Mix a small amount of royal icing with purple food colour to a soft lilac shade and put into a piping bag. Snip a small tip off the bag and pipe the drapes and loops around the sides of each cup cake. First, divide the circumference of the cup cake into 10 even sections and mark them with small dots around edge. Pipe and lift your bag from dot to dot by letting the line fall down slightly. Let the first row of swags dry.

6 Once these are completely dry, pipe the next row of swags either in between or slightly lower than the previous one. In this way you will be able to create different patterns and designs.

7 Using small dabs of icing, stick one large flower in the middle of each cup cake and the little flowers evenly around the sides of each. Then arrange the sugar pearls in the centre of each flower.

8 Mix a small amount of icing with green food colour and put it into a fresh piping bag.

9 Snip the tip off in a V shape and pipe small leaves around all the flowers. (Be careful when lifting the cakes, as the piping around the sides will be very fragile.)

White Spring Posies

This is a unique idea for little miniature wedding cakes or bridesmaids' gifts. You can use flowers to match your bridal bouquet and recreate an edible version. As these are incredibly time-consuming to make, I recommend using them for smaller weddings or events.

FOR 16 CAKES

about 1 packet (250g) of white sugar
    flower paste (Squire's Kitchen)
small amount of white vegetable fat
icing sugar or cornflour, for dusting
about 1kg white sugar paste
green food colour
16 miniature cakes (5cm/2-inch diameter),
    made from a 25cm (10 inch) square of
    basic victoria sponge mixture,
    flavoured and soaked to your choice,
    covered with marzipan and a thin layer
    of white sugar paste (see pages 122–31)
edible glue
small amount of royal icing (see page 136)

EQUIPMENT

SMALL PLASTIC BOARD
SMALL ROLLING PIN
SMALL STEPHANOTIS CUTTER
CLING FILM
STAY-FRESH MAT
FOAM PAD
FLOWER/LEAF SHAPER TOOL (PME)
CAKE SMOOTHER
SMALL KITCHEN KNIFE
SMALL ARTIST'S BRUSH
PAPER PIPING BAG (SEE PAGE 137)
PAIR OF SCISSORS

TO MAKE THE FLOWERS (YOU WILL NEED ABOUT 30 PER CAKE)

▶1 Knead the flower paste with a little white vegetable fat until smooth and pliable.

▶2 On a plastic board lightly dusted with icing sugar or cornflour, roll a small piece of flower paste out very thinly. Cut out the little flowers using the stephanotis cutter (see 1, page 63). Keep the remaining paste covered in cling film to prevent it drying out.

▶3 Keeping the flowers not being used covered with the stay-fresh mat, place a few at a time on the foam pad and push a line from the middle down each petal using the shaper tool (see 2, page 63). This way the petals will slightly curve inwards. Let dry.

▶4 Pipe little dots of royal icing into the centres of each flower (see 3, page 63). Let dry.

TO MAKE THE FLOWER STEMS

▶5 Divide the sugar paste into 4 even pieces and mix three of them with various amounts of green food colour to give 3 different shades of green. Leave the rest white.

6 To make the stems, roll a small piece of each colour green out to a thin sausage using the cake smoother, and cut into pieces long enough to cover the sides of the cakes (see 4).

7 Brush the sides of each cake with edible glue and stick the stems around in alternating shades of green (see 5). Push them flat on to the side of the cake using a cake smoother (see 6). Trim off excess at the top with a sharp knife (see 7).

TO FINISH THE TOP OF THE CAKES WITH FLOWERS

8 Roll a small piece of white sugar paste to a ball, and push it down to a dome shape. It should be large enough to cover the top of a cake. Stick it on top using a dab of royal icing (see 8). Do the same for the other cakes.

9 Using little dabs of royal icing, stick one layer of flowers all over each dome (see 9). Stick a second layer of flowers in between the gaps of the first. Let dry.

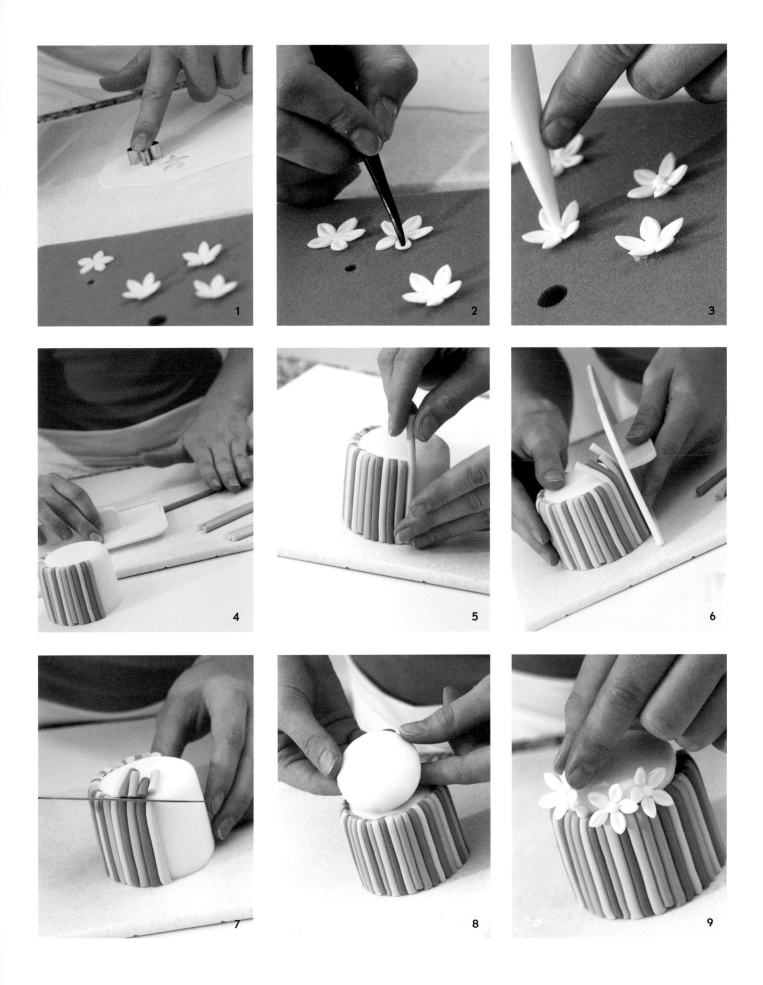

Tiffany-style Sugar Boxes

No other gift box is as recognizable as the Tiffany box.
A timeless symbol of elegance and romance and an object of desire for many,
it is often given as a wedding favour, containing a precious gift. You can,
of course, splash out and get the original; or you can make these pretty little
sugar boxes inspired by Tiffany and fill them with sugared almonds or any
gift you like. If you keep them in a dry place, they will last for months.

FOR 10 SUGAR BOXES

about 600g white sugar paste

2 teaspoons gum tragacanth

willow-green food colour (Wilton) and
    baby-blue food colour

icing sugar or cornflour for dusting

edible glue

white edible lustre

small amount of royal icing (see page 136)

EQUIPMENT

SMALL NON-STICK PLASTIC BOARD

CLING FILM

SMALL ROLLING PIN

SMALL KITCHEN KNIFE

2 CUBES OF POLYSTYRENE, ONE ABOUT 5CM
    (2 INCHES), THE OTHER JUST SLIGHTLY LARGER

SMALL BRUSH

KITCHEN PAPER

PAPER PIPING BAG (SEE PAGE 137)

PAIR OF SCISSORS

1 Mix the sugar paste with the gum tragacanth and knead it until smooth and pliable.
Colour half of the paste with a little green and blue to make a Tiffany blue as shown.
Cover this and the other piece of paste separately with cling film and let them rest for
about half an hour until the paste feels flexible and stretchy.

2 On a plastic board dusted with icing sugar or cornflour, roll out a piece of green
sugar paste to a thickness of about 3mm (⅛ inch). Turn it over and cut out a square large
enough to cover the base of the smaller polystyrene cube. Mark a square in the middle
for the base and cut an incision down to each corner as shown on page 66.

3 Lift the paste off the board, dust the cube well with icing sugar or cornflour and lay
the paste over its top so that all 4 'walls' of the sugar paste are falling down the sides.
Thinly brush the edges with edible glue and stick the sides together. Let it dry in this
position for a couple of hours.

4 Once it is almost dry, carefully remove the paste from the template so that the inside
can dry. Make 9 more in the same way.

5 Repeat the procedure using the larger polystyrene cube as a guide, but only going one-third of the way down the sides with the paste to make 10 'lids'.

6 While the bases and lids are drying, make the white sugar bows. On the plastic board dusted with icing sugar or cornflour, thinly roll out the white paste and cut it into strips about 15mm (⅝ inch) wide. You will need one strip about 8cm (3¼ inches) in length and one about 3cm (1¼ inches) in length. Brush both with white edible lustre on one side.

7 Turn the longer strip over so the lustre is facing down, fold both ends over to the middle and glue them down, supporting the loops of the bow with kitchen paper. Fold the shorter strip over the join and fix it with some edible glue. Let dry.

8 Once the box bases and lids are dry, lay a strip of white paste down each side of the boxes for the sugar ribbons. Make sure the ribbons of the lids join with the ribbons of the base when putting them together.

9 Cut out the 2 short pieces for the bow endings and stick them on top of the lid. Place the bow on top. Let dry.

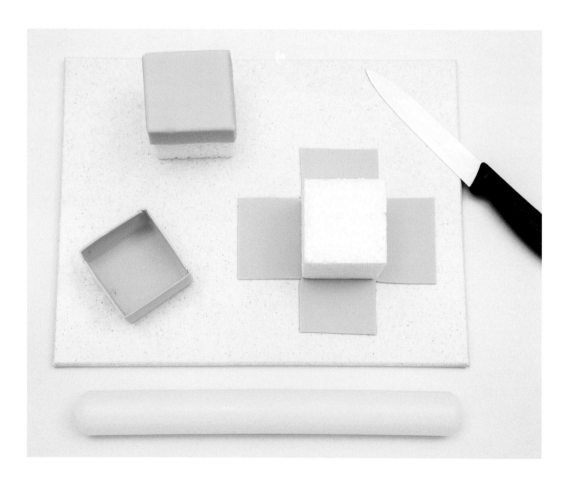

Spring Blossom Cup Cakes

Delicately handcrafted pastel-coloured spring flowers give these delicious chocolate cup cakes a fresh and romantic look. They look particularly pretty arranged on a vintage-style cake stand and are ideal for a spring wedding in a beautiful country garden.

FOR 12 CUP CAKES

about 150g white sugar flower paste

small amount of white vegetable fat

violet, dusky-pink, green and yellow food colours

icing sugar or cornflour for dusting

small amount of royal icing (see page 136)

yellow blossom tint dusting colour

12 cup cakes made using ½ recipe quantity of rich dark chocolate sponge (see page 124), baked in silver muffin cases (see pages 133–4) and iced with about 250g chocolate ganache (see page 126)

EQUIPMENT

CLING FILM

NON-STICK BOARD WITH HOLES (CELBOARD)

SMALL ROLLING PIN

SMALL PETUNIA CUTTER

FLOWER FOAM PAD WITH HOLES (CELPAD)

BONE TOOL (PME OR JEM)

VEINING TOOL (JEM)

PETAL FLUTING/POINTED END TOOL (JEM)

SMALL BOWLS

PALETTE KNIFE

PAPER PIPING BAGS (SEE PAGE 137)

SMALL STAR PIPING TUBE

SMALL PRIMROSE CUTTER

COCKTAIL STICK OR CELSTICK

VIOLET CUTTER

SERRATED AND TAPER CONE TOOL (PME)

STAYFRESH MULTI MAT

1 Knead the sugar flower paste with a small amount of white vegetable fat until smooth and pliable. Divide it into 3 equal parts and mix one with violet and one with dusky pink to a light pastel shade. Keep the 3 pieces of paste separate, covered in cling film until later use.

FOR THE PETUNIAS

2 On the part of the plastic board with the largest hole, dusted with icing sugar, roll a small amount of the dusky-pink paste out until very thin. Turn the paste upside down and place the petunia cutter over the top with the knob of paste in the middle. Cut out the

flower shape and transfer it on to the foam pad, placing the knob of paste inside the large hole.

▶3 Gently run the bone tool over the edges and then roll the veining tool across each petal. Gently shape the centre of the flower around the bone tool and slightly curve the petals with your fingers. Repeat for about 12 petunias and let dry, keeping the rest of the paste covered with cling film.

▶4 Once they are dry, mix a small amount of royal icing with green food colour and put it in a piping bag fitted with a star piping tube. Pipe a small star inside the well of each flower.

▶5 Mix a small amount of royal icing with yellow food colour. Put it in a piping bag, cut off a small tip and pipe little yellow dots for the stamens on top of the green centres. Let dry.

FOR THE PRIMROSES

6 On the part of the plastic board with the medium-size hole, lightly dusted with icing sugar, roll out a small amount of the white sugar flower paste thinly. Turn the paste upside down and place the primrose cutter over the top with the knob of paste in the middle. Cut out the flower shape and transfer it to the foam pad, placing the knob of paste inside the medium-size hole.

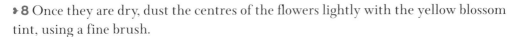

7 Using a cocktail stick or Celstick, roll over each petal to stretch it. Pick up the flower with your fingers and gently push the serrated tip of the taper cone tool into the centre of the primrose. Repeat for about 24 primroses and let dry.

8 Once they are dry, dust the centres of the flowers lightly with the yellow blossom tint, using a fine brush.

9 Mix a small amount of icing with green food colour, put it in a piping bag and pipe a small dot into the centre of each primrose.

FOR THE VIOLETS

10 On the part of the plastic board with the smallest hole, lightly dusted with icing sugar, roll out a small amount of the violet sugar flower paste thinly. Turn the paste upside down and place the violet cutter over the top with the knob of paste in the middle.

11 Cut out the flower shape and transfer it on to the foam pad with the knob of paste facing up. Gently run the bone tool from the outer edge of each petal towards the middle. This will curve up the petals.

12 Pick up the violet blossom with your fingers and gently push the smooth end of the taper cone tool into the flower centre. Repeat for about 36 violets. Let dry.

TO FINISH

13 Mix a small amount of royal icing with yellow food colour and pipe a small dot into the middle of each flower, covering the hole.

14 Once all the flowers are dry, arrange them on top of the cup cakes.

Large Cakes

American Sweet Heart

Romantically kitsch and sugary sweet, this cake of tiny little pink rosebuds
and sugar heart motifs couldn't be more appealing and girly. As such,
it is perfectly suited to something like a bridal shower party.

FOR ABOUT 70 PORTIONS

3 round cake tiers, 20cm (8 inches), 15cm
(6 inches), 10cm (4 inches) in diameter,
made from 3 ½ quantities of basic
Victoria sponge, flavoured to choice (see
pages 122–5), covered with marzipan and
then sugar paste coloured pastel pink for
top and bottom tiers, and dark pink for the
middle tier, each set on a matching thick
cake board (see pages 129–31)

100g soft-peak royal icing (see pages 136–7)

pink and green food colours

500g white sugar paste

icing sugar for dusting

edible glue or clear alcohol

EQUIPMENT

SMALL PLASTIC BOARD

SMALL ROLLING PIN

SMALL KITCHEN KNIFE

PAPER PIPING BAGS (SEE PAGE 137)

SMALL PALETTE KNIFE

SMALL BOWL

PAIR OF SCISSORS

HEART-SHAPED COOKIE CUTTER (ABOUT
5CM/2-INCH DIAMETER)

SMALL BRUSH

8 CAKE DOWELS

SCRIBBLER (KIT BOX)

GREASEPROOF PAPER

1.5 M PINK SATIN RIBBON, 10MM WIDTH

Make and cover the three cakes at least 1 or 2 days ahead and trim the bases of the
bottom and top tiers with ribbon, securing it in place with a little royal icing.

1 Adjust the scribbler to a measure of about 2.5cm (1 inch) and carefully take it around
the middle tier as shown (see 1, page 77) to mark the top limit of the icing border.

2 Divide the soft-peak royal icing into 3 and colour it 2 shades of pink and one green,
then fill each colour into a piping bag. Place the middle cake tier on top of a piece of
greaseproof paper and pipe a row of 2cm (¾-inch) long stripes in alternating colours
around the base (see 2, page 77). Finish each strip with a dot at the bottom and the top.
Let dry. Keep some of the green-coloured icing (covered) for later use.

3 Knead the white sugar paste until it is soft and pliable. Divide it in two and then
mix each half with a different amount of pink food colour to produce two different
shades of pink.

4 On a plastic board lightly dusted with icing sugar, roll out some of the pink paste to a long thin strip, trim the edges and cut it into small pieces of about 1x4cm (½ x 1½ inches). Roll each strip up into a little bud and let them dry (see 3–5). You will need about 250 dark-pink buds and 20 pale-pink buds.

5 Roll the remaining pale-pink paste out to about a thickness of about 2mm (⅟₁₂ inch) and cut out heart shapes from it.

6 Lightly mark the bottom tier into 8 sections radially, like a wheel, and lightly brush the back of a heart with edible glue or clear alcohol (see 6), then stick it on to the cake at the outer part of each section (see 7).

7 Stick a row of dark-pink rosebuds around the outside of each heart, using little dabs of royal icing (see 8). Arrange the pale-pink rosebuds individually over the middle tier and the remaining dark-pink buds in clusters of 3 all over the top tier.

8 Fill the remaining green icing into a piping bag. Cut the tip off in a V shape and pipe small leaves around the rosebuds (see 9). Let dry.

9 Assemble the cakes with 4 dowels each for the bottom and middle tiers, as described on page 132.

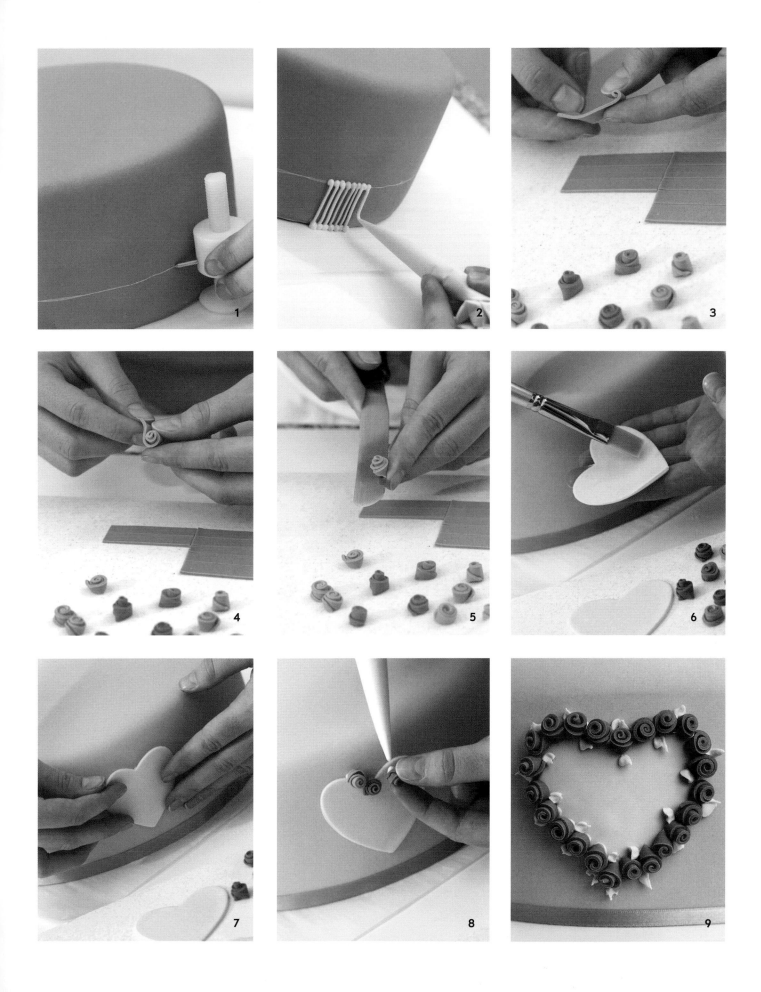

Butterfly Chocolate Cake

This clever and simple design is ideal for a not-so-traditional wedding.
Chocolate brown combined with muted pastel colours
is a very modish look right now. Some of my favourite pastels
to use in this way are dusky pink, sage green or taupe.

FOR 120 PORTIONS

small amount of white vegetable fat

about 300g royal icing (see page 136)

dark-brown and blue food colours

3 round cake tiers 25cm (10 inches), 17.5cm
(7 inches) and 10cm (4 inches), made from
6 quantities rich dark chocolate cake (see
page 124) layered with ganache (see page
126), iced with marzipan and dark-brown
chocolate-flavoured sugar paste (see pages
129–30), assembled on a 35cm (14-inch)
round cake board covered in dark-brown
chocolate-flavoured sugar paste (page 131)

EQUIPMENT

SHEET OF CELLOPHANE

SMALL BOWLS

SMALL PALETTE KNIFE

PAPER PIPING BAGS (SEE PAGE 137)

PAIR OF SCISSORS

PIECE OF THIN CARDBOARD

GREASEPROOF PAPER

ABOUT 3 M CHOCOLATE-BROWN
GROSGRAIN RIBBON, 15MM WIDTH

METAL PIN

Make the butterflies 2 days ahead.

1 Rub a very thin layer of vegetable fat over a sheet of cellophane. Lay it on top of the
butterfly template (see the inside front cover) and, using soft-peak (see page 137)
chocolate-brown royal icing, pipe the outline of the wings (see 1). Let dry.

2 When dry, flood the wing centres with blue-coloured runny icing (see page 137 and
2-3) and let dry overnight.

▸3 Once the blue icing is completely dry, decorate the wings with small dots in soft-peak chocolate-brown icing. Let dry.

▸4 Fold a piece of cardboard to a V shape to support the wings when sticking them together and line it with a piece of greaseproof paper.

▸5 Pipe a short line of soft-peak chocolate-brown icing into the fold of the paper. Lift the wings off the cellophane and stick them into the brown icing (see 1 and 2). Pipe the body down the centre of the wings over the original brown icing (see 3). Let dry overnight.

TO DECORATE THE CAKE

▸6 Cut the ribbon into 4 pieces to cover the base of each tier and the cake board. Fix the ribbon around the board with a pin and the ribbon around the cake tiers with dabs of stiff-peak chocolate-brown icing (see page 137).

▸7 Using soft-peak blue royal icing, pipe small dots evenly around each side of the ribbon and around the edge of the cake board.

▸8 Arrange the butterflies all over the cake, fixing them in place with dabs of stiff chocolate-brown icing.

Brush-embroidered Daisy Cake

To create a vintage-style look here, I used a technique called
'brush embroidery' for which I painted the daisy design on the cake with a
brush, using very lightly coloured royal icing.

FOR 70 PORTIONS

3 round cake tiers, 20cm (8 inches), 15cm
    (6 inches) and 10cm (4 inches) in diameter,
    made from 3 ½ recipe quantities of basic
    Victoria sponge, flavoured to your choice
    (see pages 122–5) and covered
    with marzipan (see pages 129–30)

2kg ready-made ivory sugar paste

100g white sugar flower paste

small amount of white vegetable fat

cornflour for dusting

about 300g soft-peak royal icing (see pages
    136–7)

yellow and green food colours

EQUIPMENT

LARGE AND SMALL ROLLING PINS

2 CAKE SMOOTHERS

DAISY PATCHWORK CUTTERS (MARION FROST)

VEINED DAISY PLUNGER CUTTER (PME)

SMALL NON-STICK PLASTIC BOARD

FLOWER FOAM PAD OR CELPAD

STAYFRESH MULTI MAT

CELSTICK OR COCKTAIL STICK

COLOUR MIXING PALETTE

SMALL BOWLS

PALETTE KNIFE

PAPER PIPING BAGS (SEE PAGE 137)

PAIR OF SCISSORS

FINE ARTIST'S BRUSHES

8 CAKE DOWELS

5MM (¼-INCH) MARZIPAN SPACERS

Make and cover the cakes 1 or 2 days ahead.

EMBOSSING THE CAKE

▶1 Cover each cake with the ivory sugar paste as described on pages 129–30.

▶2 While the sugar paste is still soft, gently impress the daisy patchwork cutters into it
to create the embossing (see 1 overleaf). Let the sugar paste dry overnight.

MAKING THE DAISY FLOWERS

▶3 In the meantime, make the daisy flowers. Mix the sugar flower paste with a small
amount of white vegetable fat and knead it until it is smooth and pliable.

4 On a plastic board dusted with cornflour, roll out the paste until very thin. Using the daisy plunger cutter, cut out 5 daisies and place one flower at a time on the foam pad. Keep the others covered with the multi mat.

5 Roll the cel stick or cocktail stick over each petal to stretch it. Then carefully lay it over the well of a colour mixing palette and push the middle down with a small rolling pin (see 2). Let it dry. Repeat for the remaining daisies.

6 Once dry, colour some of the soft-peak royal icing yellow and pipe small dots into the flowers' centres. Reserve the rest of the yellow icing for later.

BRUSH-EMBROIDERING THE CAKE

7 Divide the remaining icing in half and colour one half very pale green. Start with the green leaves. Pipe the outline using soft peak white icing for the outside and a very pale green soft-peak icing for the inside of the leaf shape. Take a fine artist's brush dampened with water and pull it from the outside to the middle of the leaf, which will create the leaf veins (see 3). Repeat with all the leaves, cleaning your brush from time to time.

8 When finished with the leaves, pipe the white outline for the daisy petals and again brush the icing from the outside edge towards the petal centre with a damp brush. Repeat for all the daisy petals, cleaning your brush from time to time. For the centres, pipe little dots of the yellow icing into the middle of each daisy.

9 Once the icing is dry, assemble the cakes with 4 dowels between each tier as described on pages 132–3.

10 With the remaining white icing, pipe small dots with a 1cm (¼-inch) gap between them around the base of each tier.

11 Arrange the daisies on top of the cake, fixing them in place with a dab of icing.

Bed of Roses

I was commissioned to create a 3-foot square version of this amazing cake
for a wedding. It was a big challenge, as I had to make over 1,500 roses to cover
such a huge area. After days of making roses, I finally delivered the cake
to the venue, utterly exhausted, with swollen hands and covered in glitter.
But I was really proud of my achievement. The Bed of Roses made an
enormous impact and everyone who saw it was stunned. Since then, it has
become one of my best-selling creations and deserves a place in this book
as one of the most romantic cakes I have ever designed.

FOR ABOUT 40-60 PORTIONS

900g red sugar paste

small amount of royal icing (see page 136)

about 2kg marzipan

red food colour

icing sugar for dusting

magenta Hologram Glitter Sparkle (EdAble Art)

one 20cm (8-inch) square single layer sponge
  cake, using 1 recipe quantity of basic
  Victoria sponge mixture, flavoured to your
  choice (see pages 122–3), covered with red
  marzipan (see pages 129–30)

EQUIPMENT

25CM (12-INCH) SQUARE CAKE BOARD

ABOUT 1.2 M FUCHSIA-PINK RIBBON, 15MM WIDTH

METAL PIN

SMALL PALETTE KNIFE

PAPER PIPING BAG (SEE PAGE 137)

PAIR OF SCISSORS

CLING FILM

2 SHEETS OF CELLOPHANE

Prepare the cake board 2 or 3 days in advance and make your roses at least one day ahead.

1 Cover the cake board with the red sugar paste and decorate the sides with fuchsia
ribbon as described on page 129–31.

2 Spread a thin layer of royal icing in the middle of the iced cake board and place the
cake on top. Let dry.

3 Colour the marzipan deep red. Keep it covered in cling film to prevent it drying out.

To make the rosebuds – you also need a rosebud as the heart of each larger rose
(the number of roses you need to cover this cake depends on the size of your roses.
For the cake illustrated, I used about 80 small rosebuds and about 20 larger open roses.

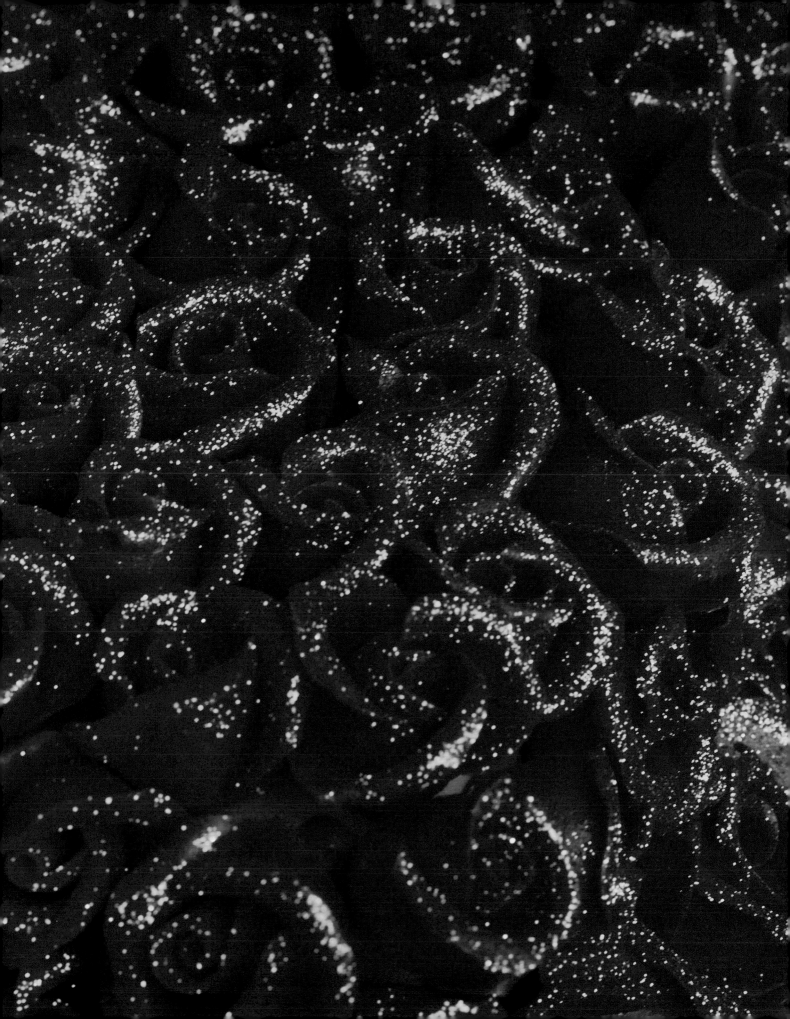

4 For each rosebud, you need 3 hazelnut-sized balls of marzipan and one twice as large.

5 Place these pieces of marzipan between two sheets of cellophane (see 1) and start with the larger one by pushing it down sideways to make it longer, and then flatten one long side with your thumb until it is very thin (see 2). Dusting the marzipan with icing sugar helps prevent it sticking.

6 For the other 2 petals, begin to push one of the smaller balls down with your thumb, starting from the centre to one side, until it forms a round petal, with one thick and one thin side. Repeat with the other balls.

7 Take the large petal first and roll it into a spiral shape, thin side up (see 3). This will form the centre of the rose.

8 Take one of the smaller petals, thin side up, and lay it around the centre over the seam (see 4).

9 Then tuck the third petal slightly inside the second petal and squeeze it around the centre (see 5).

10 Slightly curve the edge of the petals out with your fingertips (see 6).

To make the larger open roses

11 To make each large open rose, continue by laying another 3 petals of the same size around a rosebud, each slightly overlapping the other.

12 Again, slightly curve the edge of the petals outs with your fingertips to make larger roses.

13 Continue by laying another 5 petals of the same size around the rosebud, each slightly overlapping the other.

14 Slightly curve the edge of the petals out with your fingertips.

15 Pinch excess marzipan off the bottom of each rose (see 8).

To finish the decorations

16 While still wet, dip the finished roses into the glitter sparkle (see 9), then let the roses dry overnight.

17 Once dry, stick the roses on the cake with red icing, first arranging the large roses around the sides and then putting the small buds all over the top.

My Fair Lady Cake

As the name suggests, the inspiration for this cake comes from
the famous Ascot scene designed by Cecil Beaton for the musical
My Fair Lady. Black and white is currently much in vogue for urban
weddings, so this cake design is proving very popular.

FOR 70 PORTIONS

500g sugar flower paste

small amount of white vegetable fat

cornflour for dusting

edible glue

small amount of royal icing (see page 136)

black food colour

icing sugar for dusting

3 round cake tiers, 20cm (8 inches), 15cm (6
   inches) and 10cm (4 inches) in diameter,
   made from 3 ½ recipe quantities of basic
   Victoria sponge, flavoured to your choice
   (see pages 122–3), iced with marzipan and
   white sugar paste (see pages 129–30)

1 kg white sugar paste

EQUIPMENT

SMALL NON-STICK PLASTIC BOARD

SMALL ROLLING PIN

CLING FILM

LARGE AND MEDIUM ROSE PETAL CUTTER (FMM)

FLOWER FOAM PAD

STAYFRESH MULTI MAT

BONE TOOL AND VEINING TOOL (JEM)

SMALL COLOUR PALETTE

SMALL PALETTE KNIFE

PAPER PIPING BAGS (SEE PAGE 137)

KITCHEN KNIFE

RULER

SMALL PASTRY BRUSH

8 CAKE DOWELS

STRONG PAIR OF SCISSORS

Make your flowers at least one day ahead. You will need about 28 flowers for this cake.

1 Knead the sugar flower paste with a small
amount of vegetable fat until smooth and pliable.

2 On the plastic board lightly dusted with
cornflour, roll out a small amount of flower paste
until very thin, keeping the rest covered with
cling film so it doesn't dry out. First, cut out a large
shape using the large rose petal cutter and place
it on the foam pad.

3 Run the thick end of the bone tool along the
edges until they become thin and slightly frilly.
Then roll the veining tool across each petal.

4 Place the flower in the well of a cornflour-dusted painter's palette. Push the middle down with the end of the rolling pin and let dry. Repeat for all 28 flowers. Let dry.

5 Once these are dry, repeat steps 2 to 4 using the medium rose petal cutter and place on top of the larger dry ones. Fix the flower centres in place with edible glue. Let dry.

6 Once these are dry, pipe small dots of black royal icing into the flower centres.

COVERING THE CAKES WITH STRIPES

7 Knead the sugar paste until smooth and pliable. Divide in half and colour one piece deep black. Cover it with cling film and let it rest for about 1 hour.

8 On a clean surface dusted with icing sugar, roll out one piece of white and one piece of black sugar paste, both of the same size and about 3mm (⅛ inch) thick. Trim the edges and cut each piece into strips of about 4x10cm (1½x4 inches).

9 Stick the strips on the side of each cake in alternating colours (see 1), using edible glue to fix them in place. Trim any excess paste off the top, using a kitchen knife (see 2) and push them flat on the sides using a cake smoother (see 3). Let dry.

10 Once these are dry, assemble the cake tiers, using the dowels and the instructions on page 132, as well as the dowel template on the inside back cover, to support the tiers.

1

2

3

Neapolitan Monogrammed Cake

Use this very graphic and contemporary design to make your
own signature cake by incorporating the initials of the bride and groom.
Chocolate-brown and cream combine well with any pastel colour,
such as blue, sage green or caramel.

FOR ABOUT 225 PORTIONS

about 2kg dark-brown chocolate-flavoured
   sugar paste
icing sugar for dusting
2 round cake tiers, 10cm (4 inches) and 35cm
   (14 inches) in diameter, made from 9
   recipe quantities of basic Victoria sponge,
   flavoured to your choice (see pages
   122–3), covered with marzipan and then
   with sugar paste that has been coloured
   pastel pink (see pages 129–30)
one 17.5cm (7-inch) round cake tier, made
   from 1½ recipe quantities of basic
   Victoria sponge, flavoured to your
   choice (see pages 122–3), covered with
   marzipan and then with sugar paste that has
   been coloured ivory (see pages 129–30)
one 25cm (10-inch) round cake tier, made
   from 4 recipe quantities of basic
   Victoria sponge, flavoured to your choice
   (see pages 122–3), covered with marzipan
   and then with dark brown chocolate-
   flavoured sugar paste (see pages 129–30)
edible glue or alcohol
about 300g royal icing (see page 136)
ivory, pink and dark-brown food colours
about 150g pastel-pink sugar paste

EQUIPMENT

45CM (18-INCH) ROUND THICK CAKE BOARD
SMALL PALETTE KNIFE
SMALL NON-STICK PLASTIC BOARD
SMALL ROLLING PIN
ROUND PASTRY CUTTERS (3CM AND 5CM)
SMALL BOWLS
PAPER PIPING BAGS (SEE PAGE 137)
PAIR OF SCISSORS
CLING FILM
SMALL BRUSH
TILTING TURNTABLE
14 PLASTIC CAKE DOWELS
PAIR OF STRONG SCISSORS
2.5 M CHOCOLATE-BROWN SATIN RIBBON,
   7MM WIDTH
1.5 M CHOCOLATE-BROWN SATIN RIBBON,
   15MM WIDTH
60CM IVORY SATIN RIBBON, 7MM WIDTH
METAL PIN

Make and cover the cake tiers at least 1 or 2 days ahead.

1 Cover the cake board with about 1.5kg dark-brown chocolate-flavoured sugar paste. Let dry overnight.

2 Spread a thin layer of royal icing into the middle of the iced cake board and place the largest tier on top of it.

3 On a plastic board dusted with icing sugar, roll out the rest of the brown sugar paste thinly and cut out circles using a 3cm round cutter. Stick them evenly spaced around the sides of the largest tier, using edible glue or alcohol to fix them in place.

4 Using soft-peak ivory royal icing (see page 137), pipe a row of tiny dots around each circle, then pipe another row of dots between every other one of the first row.

5 For the 17.5cm (7-inch) ivory cake, repeat the same process using pastel-pink sugar paste, a 5cm round cutter and brown icing for piping the dots. Let dry before piping on the monograms.

6 To pipe the monograms, place the cake on top of a turntable slightly tilted away from you. Using brown soft-peak royal icing, write the monograms into the middle of the pink circles.

7 Place the 25cm (10-inch) brown cake on top of the turntable. Mark the side of the cake evenly into sections about 5cm wide with tiny dots of icing. Slightly tilt the turntable away from you. With a piping bag filled with pink soft-peak icing, pipe a drape from one mark to another, turning the cake as required.

8 Now pipe 3 small loops above each join and finish the design with little piped dots.

9 Repeat steps 7 and 8 for the pink top tier cake using dark-brown icing.

10 Push 6 dowels into the bottom tier and 4 dowels each into the 25 cm (10-inch) and 17.5cm (7-inch) cakes, using the dowel template on the inside back cover, and assemble the cake following the instructions on page 132.

11 Arrange the ribbons around the base of each tier, fixing the ends with icing and around the cake board, fixing the ends with a metal pin.

White Blossom Abundance

This design is ideal for beginners, as the sides of the cake are completely covered with flowers, so any little cracks in the icing can be perfectly hidden. You do need good piping skills to make the sugar flowers, but you can make them out of flower paste instead, using a simple five-petal flower cutter to achieve a very similar look.

FOR ABOUT 200 **PORTIONS**

about 1kg royal icing (see page 136)

ivory food colour

4 round cake tiers, 30cm (12 inches), 25cm (10 inches), 20cm (8 inches) and 15cm (6 inches) in diameter, made from 13 ½ recipe quantities of basic Victoria sponge, flavoured to your choice (see pages 122–3), covered with marzipan and then with ivory sugar paste (see pages 129–30)

35cm (14 inch) round cake board covered with ivory sugar paste (see page 131)

EQUIPMENT

GREASEPROOF PAPER

PAPER PIPING BAGS (SEE PAGE 137)

PAIR OF SCISSORS

SELECTION OF PETAL PIPING TUBES (I USE WILTON 102, 103 AND 104)

FLOWER NAIL

SMALL PALETTE KNIFE

SMALL BOWL

14 PLASTIC CAKE DOWELS

PAIR OF STRONG SCISSORS OR SMALL SAW

10CM (4-INCH), 15CM (6-INCH), 20CM (8-INCH) AND 25CM (10-INCH) ROUND THICK CAKE BOARDS

2.5M IVORY SATIN RIBBON, 15MM WIDTH

CLING FILM OR DAMP CLOTH

5 METAL PINS

Make the flowers 1 or 2 days ahead. The number of flowers you will need depends on how large you pipe them. I used about 300 flowers in three different sizes for this cake.

1 From a sheet of greaseproof paper, cut small squares slightly larger than the flower you want to pipe.

2 Make a paper piping bag and snip the tip off the empty bag to produce an opening large enough to fit a metal piping tube. Drop a Wilton 104 or PME 58R piping nozzle inside the bag, narrow end first.

3 Fill the bag with stiff-peak plain white royal icing (see pages 136–7).

4 Pipe a small dot of icing on top of the flower nail, stick one of the paper squares on top and hold the nail in one hand.

5 Hold the piping bag in the other hand at a 45-degree angle to the nail, with the wide end touching the centre of the flower nail and the narrow end pointing out and slightly raised.

6 Squeeze out the first petal and give the nail a one-fifth turn as you move the nozzle out towards the edge of the flower nail. Use less pressure as you are moving back towards the centre and curve the nozzle slightly to give the petal a natural shape. Stop squeezing as the wide end touches the centre of the nail and lift up the nozzle.

7 Repeat this 4 more times to make all the petals.

8 Remove the flower with its base paper from the nail and leave it to dry.

9 Colour some icing ivory and pipe small ivory dots into the centres as stamens.

10 Let the flowers dry in a warm place overnight.

TO DECORATE THE CAKE

11 Once all the flowers are dry, stick them around the sides of each tier with dabs of royal icing. Mix the different sizes and use the smallest flowers to fill the gaps. Let dry.

12 Push 6 dowels into the largest cake and 4 dowels each into the 25cm (10-inch) and 20cm (8-inch) cake, using the dowel template on the inside back cover and the instructions on page 132.

13 Cut the ribbon into 5 pieces long enough to cover the base board and the separator boards. Arrange them around each board and fix the ends with metal pins.

14 Stack the cakes on top of each other with a separator board in between each tier, starting with the largest cake board and cake at the bottom. Spread a small amount of royal icing between each tier and board to stabilize the construction.

Homage to Cath Kidston

I am a big fan of Cath Kidston's work and this wedding cake was inspired by some of her fabric and wallpaper designs. The mix of different patterns and cake shapes works particularly well, as I have tied them together by repeating colours and textures on every other tier. I have topped the cake with a crown of large handcrafted roses in luscious red with cerise-pink centres, which you can make well in advance.

FOR 320 PORTIONS

about 1.5kg ready-made pastel-pink sugar paste

about 250g sugar flower paste

red, pink and green food colours

ruby blossom tint dusting colour (Sugar Flair)

small amount of white vegetable fat

about 1kg royal icing (see page 136)

2 cake tiers, 35cm (14 inches) and 25cm (10 inches) square, made from 12 ½ recipe quantities of basic Victoria sponge, flavoured to your choice (see pages 122–3), both covered with marzipan and then ivory and pastel-pink sugar paste respectively (see pages 129–30)

2 round cake tiers, 17.5cm (7 inches) and 10cm (4 inches), made from 2 recipe quantities of basic Victoria sponge, flavoured to your choice (see pages 122–3), both covered with marzipan and then ivory and pastel-pink sugar paste respectively (see pages 129–30)

edible glue

cornflour for dusting

EQUIPMENT

TWO 45CM (18-INCH) SQUARE THICK CAKE BOARDS STUCK TOGETHER WITH ROYAL ICING

CAKE SMOOTHER

SELECTION OF FINE ARTIST'S BRUSHES

ROLLING PIN

ROSE PETAL CUTTER SET

ROSE LEAF CUTTERS

ROSE LEAF VEINING MAT

CALYX CUTTERS, LARGE AND SMALL

SMALL NON-STICK PLASTIC BOARD

STAYFRESH MULTI MAT

FLOWER FOAM PAD

SMALL ROLLING PIN

BONE TOOL

SHEETS OF CELLOPHANE

PAPER PIPING BAGS (SEE PAGE 137)

2.5 M IVORY SATIN RIBBON, 15MM WIDTH, FOR THE 35CM (14-INCH), 17.5CM (7-INCH) AND 10CM (4-INCH) CAKE TIERS

TILTING TURNTABLE

1.85 M PINK MICRODOT RIBBON, 25MM WIDTH, FOR THE 45CM (18-INCH) SQUARE CAKE BOARD

METAL PIN

19 CAKE DOWELS

Cover the double cake board and make the roses about 2 days ahead.

1 Cover the double cake board with pastel-pink sugar paste as described on page 131. Let dry.

2 Using cerise-pink sugar flower paste for the rose centres and deep red for the outer petals, make about 6 large open roses, 5 small rosebuds and a couple of green leaves as described on pages 139–41. Dust and steam the finished roses with ruby blossom tint as described on page 141.

Make the rose runouts the day before.

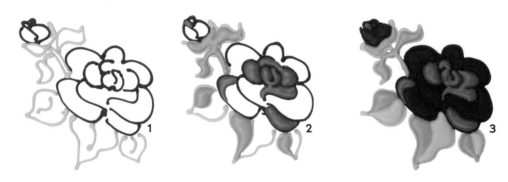

3 Place a sheet of cellophane, very thinly greased with vegetable fat, on top of the template on the inside front cover. Using a paper icing bag of red soft-peak royal icing, trace the outlines of the petals and do the same with the leaves using green icing (see 1). Repeat piping the outlines of the template 4 times, one for each side. Let dry.

4 Once the outlines have dried, flood the centres of the roses with runny pink and red icing, and the leaves with 2 shades of green icing (see 2 and 3). Let dry overnight.

DECORATE THE PINK CAKE TIERS

5 Arrange ribbon around the base of the 10cm (4-inch) top tier, held in place with a dab of icing, and pipe small ivory dots all over it. Let dry.

6 Place the 25cm (10-inch) tier on top of the turntable, slightly tilted away from you. Using ivory soft-peak icing, pipe thin lines evenly from the top edge down to the bottom of the cake. You can use a smaller square cake board to act as a guide as shown. Let dry.

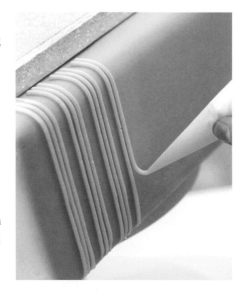

TO ASSEMBLE AND FINISH

7 Arrange the pink microdot ribbon around the side of the 45cm (18-inch) double cake board and fix the ends with a metal pin at the back.

8 Spread a thin layer of icing into the middle of the base board and carefully put the 35cm (14-inch) bottom tier in place. Cut a piece of ivory satin ribbon long enough to cover the sides of the cake and lay it around the base. Fix the ends with a small dab of icing. Arrange the rose runouts for the bottom tier all around the sides, fixing them in place with icing.

9 Arrange another piece of ivory satin ribbon around the base of the 17.5cm (7-inch) ivory cake and stick on the little rose runouts with icing.

10 To assemble the cake, use 9 dowels for the bottom tier and 5 each for the second and third, as described on page 132 and using the dowel template on the inside back cover.

11 Once the cake tiers have been stacked on top of one another, arrange the roses and leaves on the top tier, using stiff royal icing to fix them in place.

Something Borrowed, Something Blue...

We normally think of accessories when it comes to this famous tradition. But why not reflect something borrowed and something blue on the cake by using some old family jewellery and blue satin bows?

FOR 250 PORTIONS

small amount of royal icing (see page 136)

ivory food colour

4 round cake tiers, 35cm (14 inches), 27.5cm (11 inches), 20cm (8 inches) and 12.5cm (5 inches), made from 16 quantities of basic Victoria sponge, flavoured to your choice (see pages 122–3), iced with marzipan and ivory sugar paste (see pages 129–30), assembled (see page 132) on a 35cm (18-inch) double round cake board covered with ivory sugar paste (see page 131) and 60cm ivory satin ribbon

icing sugar for dusting

100g white sugar paste

white pearl lustre powder

edible glue or clear alcohol

EQUIPMENT

12 PLASTIC DOWELS

SMALL BOWLS

SMALL PALETTE KNIFE

PAPER PIPING BAG (SEE PAGE 137)

ABOUT 3 M BLUE SATIN RIBBON, 70MM WIDTH

2 PIECES OF JEWELLERY SUCH AS BROOCHES, IDEALLY HEIRLOOMS

PAIR OF SCISSORS

SMALL NON-STICK PLASTIC BOARD

SMALL ROLLING PIN

TEXTURED ROLLING PIN-SCROLL PATTERN (JEM)

STEPHANOTIS CUTTER

FINE ARTIST'S BRUSH

Make and cover your cakes at least 1 or 2 days ahead.

1 Once the tiers are assembled, using ivory soft-peak (see page 137) royal icing, pipe a dotted border around the base of the bottom and the third tier. Tie a blue ribbon bow around the second and the fourth tier and attach a piece of jewellery on to the middle of each bow. Trim the ribbon ends with scissors.

2 On a plastic board dusted with icing sugar, thinly roll out the sugar paste. Use the textured rolling pin to push a scroll design into the paste. Cut out about 20 stephanotis flower shapes and dust with white pearl lustre. Carefully turn them upside down and brush the backs thinly with edible glue or alcohol. Arrange in clusters cascading down the cake. Repeat until you have enough flowers to cover the cake (about 120).

3 Pipe small dots of ivory-coloured royal icing into the middle of the flowers.

Romantic Rose Cake

Luscious pinks and purples are one of my favourite colour combinations –
perfect for autumn weddings. The beauty of this cake is that you can tie it in with
the reception by matching the colour of the roses to the ones in your bouquet.

FOR 100 PORTIONS

about 300g sugar flower paste

small amount of white vegetable fat

pink, purple and green food colours

plum blossom tint dusting colour (Sugar Flair)

edible glue

about 200g sugar paste

about 1 teaspoon gum tragacanth

3 round cake tiers, 25cm (10 inches), 17.5cm
    (7 inches), 10cm (4 inches) in diameter,
    made from 6 recipe quantities of basic
    Victoria sponge, flavoured to your
    choice (see pages 122–3), iced with
    marzipan and white sugar paste (see pages
    129–30), assembled on a 35cm (14-inch)
    round cake board covered with white sugar
    paste (see page 131)

icing sugar for dusting

small amount of royal icing (see page 136)

EQUIPMENT

8 CAKE DOWELS

CLING FILM

3.2 M LILAC GROSGRAIN RIBBON, 25MM WIDTH

ROSE PETAL CUTTER SET

COCKTAIL STICKS

FINE ARTIST'S BRUSH

CAKE SMOOTHER

SMALL NON-STICK PLASTIC BOARD

SMALL ROLLING PIN

ROSE LEAF CUTTERS

ROSE LEAF VEINING MAT

PAPER PIPING BAG (SEE PAGE 137)

PAIR OF SCISSORS

Make your roses at least 2 days ahead.

1 Knead the sugar flower paste with a small amount of white vegetable fat until
smooth and pliable, then divide it into 3 equal pieces. Colour one piece of paste deep
cerise pink, one lilac (a lighter purple) and one deep purple. Keep them covered with
cling film until later use.

2 For this cake I made one large open rose, 3 open roses and 3 rosebuds (see pages
139–141), plus some extra rose petals. Dust the petals with the plum dusting colour and
steam (see page 141). Finish them off with the calyxes, gluing them in place. Let dry.

TO MAKE THE STEMS

3 Knead the sugar paste until smooth and pliable. Add some green food colour and the gum tragacanth, and mix until the paste feels slightly stretchy. Cover with cling film and let it rest for about 1 hour.

4 In the meantime, arrange the ribbon around the bottom of each tier of the cake as shown.

5 To make the stems, roll little thin sausages out of the green sugar paste, using the cake smoother. Cut them into different lengths and stick them on the sides of the cake with the edible glue.

TO MAKE THE ROSE LEAVES AND FINISH THE CAKE

6 On a plastic board lightly dusted with icing sugar, roll the remaining green paste out until very thin. Cut out different sizes of rose leaves, push them between the veiner and attach them to the stems with edible glue or royal icing.

7 Now fix the rose heads and buds at the top of the endings of the stems with a dab of royal icing. If necessary, support them with your finger until the icing sets and use cocktail sticks to hold them in place. Arrange some petals down the sides of the cake.

Basics

MAKING & BAKING

1 mixing bowl / electric mixer with paddle attachment
2 muffin cases
3 truffle dipping fork
4 large rolling pin
5 assortment of cake boards
6 assortment of cookie cutters
7 metal side scraper
8 large serrated kitchen knife
9 large palette knife
· selection of bowls
· flour / icing sugar sieve
· baking tray
· cake tins – round & square
· saucepan
· whisk
· greaseproof paper
· scissors
· rubber spatula
· pastry brush
· cooling rack
· muffin tray
· marzipan spacers / guide sticks
· tiltable turntable
· long metal palette knife
· small kitchen knife

DECORATING

10–15 artist's paint brushes
16 paper piping bags
17 selection of food colours
18 selection of edible glitter sparkle
19 selection of edible lustre powders
20 flower nail
21 assorted metal piping nozzles
22 lolly sticks
23 small rolling pin
24 small non-stick plastic board
25 flower foam pad
26 rose leaf veiner
· acetate sheet / Stay Fresh Multi Mat
· design wheeler
· crimping tool
· small painter's palette
· cake smoothers
· plastic dowels
· assorted flower-making tools
· assorted flower cutters / daisy cutter

Basic Equipment

Here I set out what I think is the basic kit you'll need to make and decorate the cakes in this book. I'm definitely not saying that you'll need to get everything on my list. You can often improvise with very basic tools that you already have in your kitchen. You also might prefer just to start with a few basics, such as a palette knife, some greaseproof paper to make piping bags, a few basic nozzles and a rolling pin, and then slowly build up your batterie de cuisine, getting a few things now and then, as and when you tackle those cakes that really need more sophisticated equipment.

6

7

8

9

16

18

19

20

21

22

23

24

Baking Basic Cookies

The recipes for cookies and cakes that I have developed during the past couple of years produce results that not only taste delicious, but also have a very good texture, and – although light – are solid enough to provide an ideal base for decoration. It is important that you follow each recipe carefully, as baking requires time and patience. As vital as it is to master the techniques, it is equally important to use only the best ingredients available, such as organic butter and eggs, real vanilla extract and high-quality preserves and liqueurs.

Basic Sugar Cookies

MAKES ABOUT 25 MEDIUM-SIZE OR 12 LARGE COOKIES

Baking temperature: 180°C, gas 4; baking time: 6–10 minutes, depending on size

200g unsalted soft butter
200g caster sugar
1 egg, lightly beaten
400g plain flour, plus more for dusting

OPTIONAL FLAVOURS

- For vanilla cookies, add seeds from 1 vanilla pod
- For lemon cookies, add finely grated zest of 1 lemon
- For orange cookies, add finely grated zest of 1 orange
- For chocolate cookies, replace 50g of the plain flour with 50g cocoa powder

EQUIPMENT

ELECTRIC MIXER WITH PADDLE ATTACHMENT
CLING FILM
5MM (¼ INCH) GUIDE STICKS
LARGE ROLLING PIN
COOKIE CUTTERS IN VARIOUS SHAPES
SMALL PALETTE KNIFE
BAKING TRAY
GREASEPROOF PAPER
WIRE COOLING RACK

▶ 1 In the electric mixer with paddle attachment, cream the butter, sugar and any flavouring until well mixed and just becoming creamy in texture. Don't overwork, or the cookies will spread during baking.

2 Beat in the egg until well combined. Sieve in the flour and mix on low speed until a dough forms (see 1). Gather it into a ball, wrap it in cling film and chill it for at least 1 hour.

3 Place the dough on a floured surface and knead it briefly. Using two 5mm (¼-inch) guide sticks, roll it out to an even thickness (see 2).

4 Use cookie cutters to cut out the desired shapes (see 3) and, using a palette knife, lay these on a baking tray lined with greaseproof paper. Chill again for about 30 minutes and preheat the oven to 180°C, gas 4.

5 Bake for 6–10 minutes. depending on size, until golden brown at the edges. Leave to cool on a wire rack. Wrapped in foil or cling film, they will keep well in a cool dry place for up to a month.

Tip: always bake equal sized cookies together to make sure they cook in the same time. If you mix different sizes, the smaller ones are already cooked when the larger ones are still raw in the middle.

Gingerbread Cookies

MAKES ABOUT 40 MEDIUM-SIZE COOKIES OR 20 LARGE ONES

Baking temperature: 200°C, gas 6; baking time: 8–12 minutes, depending on size

250g cold salted butter, diced
1 teaspoon bicarbonate of soda
560g plain flour

for the hot mix

5 tablespoons water
210g brown sugar
3 tablespoons treacle
3 tablespoons golden syrup
3 tablespoons ground ginger
3 tablespoons ground cinnamon
1 teaspoon ground cloves

EQUIPMENT

DEEP HEAVY SAUCEPAN
WOODEN SPOON OR PLASTIC SPATULA
ELECTRIC MIXER WITH PADDLE ATTACHMENT
SIEVE
CLING FILM
5MM (¼ INCH) GUIDE STICKS
ROLLING PIN
ASSORTED COOKIE CUTTERS
SMALL PALETTE KNIFE
BAKING TRAY
GREASEPROOF PAPER
WIRE COOLING RACK

1 Place all the ingredients for the hot mix in a deep heavy saucepan and bring to the boil, stirring (see 1 overleaf).

2 Once boiled, remove the pan from the heat and, using a wooden spoon or plastic spatula, carefully stir in the diced butter (see 2 overleaf).

Gingerbread Cookies *(continued)*

3 Once well combined, add the bicarbonate of soda and whisk the mix through briefly.

4 Pour into the bowl of the electric mixer and allow to cool until just slightly warm.

5 Once the mixture has cooled, sieve the flour over the top and start combining the two on a low speed, using the paddle attachment, until it forms a dough (see 3).

6 Wrap the dough in cling film and chill for a couple of hours or overnight.

7 Place the chilled dough on a floured clean surface and knead it through briefly.

8 Place the kneaded dough between two 5mm (¼ inch) guide sticks and roll it out to an even thickness.

9 Use the cookie cutters to cut out the desired shapes and lay them on a baking tray lined with greaseproof paper.

10 Chill again for about 30 minutes. Preheat the oven to 200°C, gas 6.

11 Bake the cookies in the preheated oven for about 8–12 minutes, depending on the cookie size, until just firm to the touch.

12 Lift off the tray and allow to cool on a wire rack. Wrapped in foil or cling film, they will keep well in a cool dry place for up to a month.

Tips
• Cookie dough or uncooked cookies can be wrapped in cling film and stored in the freezer for up to 3 months.
• Cookies baked from frozen hold better in shape as they don't tend to spread as much as chilled ones.
• Baked sugar cookies will keep for up to 1 month and gingerbread cookies up to 3 months, if kept in an airtight container or cookie jar.

Baking Basic Cakes

Lining a Round Cake Tin

EQUIPMENT

CAKE TIN OF THE REQUIRED SIZE

GREASEPROOF PAPER

PENCIL

PAIR OF SCISSORS

PASTRY BRUSH

VEGETABLE OIL

1 Place the cake tin on top of the greaseproof paper, draw a line around the base with a pencil and use that as a guide to cut out a piece to line the base.

2 Then cut out a strip that is about 5cm (2 inches) higher than the sides of your tin and long enough to line the inside edge. Fold 2.5cm (1 inch) of this strip over along its length and cut little snips along the folded edge up to the crease.

3. Brush the inside of the cake tin thinly with vegetable oil.

4 Place the long paper strip with the snipped edge at the bottom inside the tin to cover the sides. Brush the paper snips with a little oil.

5 Now place the paper base on top and make sure the snips and the base form a sharp corner and won't allow any mixture to leak through the paper lining.

For square tins, use the same technique as above, but fold the long strip that covers the sides at the four corners to fit neatly inside the tin (see page 123).

Tip: As sponge naturally shrinks during baking and the sides are drier than the centre of a cake, my advice is always to use a cake tin that is 2.5cm (1 inch) larger than required and then trim the edges of the baked sponge to the exact size you need.

Basic Victoria Sponge

MAKES ONE 20CM (8-INCH) SPONGE CAKE (1/2 A TIER), 25 FONDANT FANCIES OR 20-24 CUP CAKES

(For other sizes and quantities please refer to the guide on page 143.)
Baking temperature: 180°C, gas 4; baking time: 12–15 minutes for cup cakes, 25–45 minutes for large cakes, depending on size

200g salted butter, softened
200g caster sugar
4 medium eggs
200g self-raising flour
100ml sugar syrup (see page 125), flavoured to your choice

EQUIPMENT

ELECTRIC MIXER WITH PADDLE ATTACHMENT
MIXING BOWL
CAKE TIN FOR LARGE CAKE, BAKING TRAY FOR FONDANT FANCIES, MUFFIN TRAYS AND MUFFIN CASES FOR CUP CAKES
WOODEN SKEWER
GREASEPROOF PAPER
LARGE PALETTE KNIFE
SMALL SPOON OR LARGE PLASTIC PIPING BAG
WIRE COOLING RACK

Optional Flavours
• For vanilla sponge, add the seeds of 1 vanilla pod
• For lemon sponge, add the finely grated zest of 2 lemons
• For orange sponge, add the finely grated zest of 2 oranges

Tip: I recommend baking cup cakes on the same day as they will be iced, as they tend to dry out faster than large cakes.

1 Preheat the oven to 180°C, gas 4.

2 Place the butter, the sugar and any flavouring in the bowl of an electric mixer and, using the paddle attachment, cream together until pale and fluffy.

3 Beat the eggs lightly in another bowl and slowly add to the mix, while paddling on medium speed. If the mixture starts curdling, add a little bit of flour.

4 Once the eggs and butter mixture are combined, sieve in the flour at low speed.

5 Line the required baking tin as shown opposite or on page 121. For cup cakes, place the paper cases into the muffin trays.

6 Spread the dough evenly into the tin using a palette knife (see overleaf).

Tip: As sponge always rises more in the centre, spread it slightly higher around the sides. For cup cakes, fill the paper cases about two-thirds full, using a small spoon or a plastic piping bag.

7 Bake for 12–15 minutes for cup cakes and 25–45 minutes for large cakes, depending on size. The sponge is cooked when it springs back to the touch and the sides are coming away from the tin. Alternatively, you can check it by inserting a clean thin knife into the centre; it should come out clean.

8 While the sponge is baking, make your sugar syrup.

9 Once the sponge is baked, let it rest for about 15 minutes.

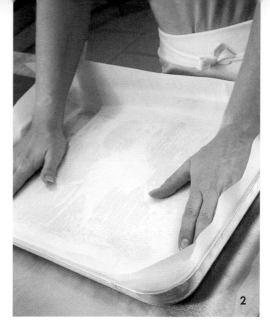

▶10 Prick the top of the sponge with a wooden skewer and, using a pastry brush, soak it with the syrup while the sponge is still warm. For cup cakes, wait about 10 minutes after baking before soaking the cup cakes with the sugar syrup. This way they will not absorb the syrup immediately and seem dry.

▶11 Once cool, remove the cake from the tin and cool on wire rack.

▶12 For large cakes, once cool, wrap the sponge in greaseproof paper, then foil. Store in a cool dry place overnight.

Tips:
• I prefer to let large sponges rest overnight as they tend to crumble if cut, layered and iced on the same day as baking.
• Sponges and cup cakes have a shelf life of up to 7 days after icing, and are suitable for freezing. If wrapped well, they can be frozen for up to 3 months.

Rich Dark Chocolate Cake

This is a little bit moister than most other chocolate cakes, but it is also denser and slightly heavier, which makes it an excellent base for tiered wedding cakes. It has a shelf life of up to 7 days after icing.

MAKES ONE 20CM (8-INCH) CAKE OR 20–24 CUP CAKES

Baking temperature: 160°C, gas 3; baking time: about 15 minutes for cup cakes, 25–45 minutes for large cakes, depending on size

75g dark couverture chocolate drops
100ml milk
225g brown sugar
75g salted butter, softened
2 medium eggs, slightly beaten
150g plain flour
1½ tablespoons cocoa powder
½ teaspoon baking powder
½ teaspoon bicarbonate of soda

EQUIPMENT
CAKE TINS FOR LARGE CAKES OR FONDANT
    FANCIES, MUFFIN TRAYS AND CASES FOR
    CUP CAKES
GREASEPROOF PAPER
DEEP SAUCEPAN
ELECTRIC MIXER WITH PADDLE ATTACHMENT
SIEVE
MIXING BOWL
MEASURING JUG
RUBBER SPATULA OR WOODEN SPOON

For other sizes and quantities, please refer to the guide on page 143.

1 Preheat the oven to 160°C, gas 3.

2 Line the required baking tin as described on page 121. For cup cakes place the muffin paper cases into the muffin trays.

3 Place the chocolate, milk and half of the sugar into a deep saucepan and bring to the boil, while stirring occasionally.

4 Using an electric mixer with a paddle attachment, beat the butter and the remaining sugar until pale and fluffy.

5 Slowly add the eggs.

6 Sift the flour, cocoa powder, baking powder and bicarbonate of soda and add to the mixture while mixing at a low speed.

7 While the chocolate mix is still hot, using a measuring jug, slowly pour it into the dough while mixing at low speed.

8 Once combined, pour the mixture from the bowl directly into the lined tin. For cup cakes, first transfer the cake mix into a measuring jug, as it is very liquid, and use to fill the paper cases about two-thirds full.

9 Bake for 15 minutes for cup cakes, 25–45 minutes for large cakes, depending on size. It is cooked when it springs back to the touch and the sides are coming away from the tin. Or, insert a clean thin knife into the centre; it should come out clean.

10 Once the cake is baked, let it rest for about 15 minutes. Once cool, remove from the tin.

11 For storage, wrap in greaseproof paper, then in foil and store in a cool dry place overnight. This cake is suitable for freezing. Wrapped well, it can be frozen for up to 3 months.

Cake Fillings

Sugar Syrups

MAKES 100ML SUGAR SYRUP - roughly the amount needed for a 20cm (8-inch) layered cake tier, a 30cm (12-inch) single-tier square sponge to make 25 fondant fancies, or 20–24 cup cakes

For vanilla syrup

5 tablespoons water

75g sugar

seeds from ½ vanilla pod or 1 teaspoon
    Madagascan vanilla essence

For lemon syrup

5 tablespoons freshly squeezed lemon juice

75g sugar

1 tablespoon Limoncello liqueur

For orange syrup

5 tablespoons freshly squeezed orange juice

75g sugar

1 tablespoon Grand Marnier liqueur

EQUIPMENT

DEEP SAUCEPAN

SPATULA

1 Place the water or juice and sugar in a deep saucepan and bring to the boil. Remove from the heat and allow it to cool.

2 Once cool, stir in the flavourings.

3 Ideally, let the syrup infuse overnight as this will bring out the most in the flavours.

4 To store sugar syrup, keep it in an airtight bottle or container inside the fridge and it will last for up to 1 month.

Buttercream Frosting

Following a traditional English recipe, I use equal quantities of butter and icing sugar to make my buttercream. The method is very simple and, as it is an egg-free recipe, it has a longer shelf life than most other buttercreams.

MAKES 600G – roughly the amount you will need to layer a 20cm (8-inch) cake tier or 25 small cakes

300g unsalted butter, softened

300g icing sugar, sifted

pinch of salt

For other sizes and quantities please refer to the guide on page 143.

Optional Flavours

- For vanilla buttercream, add the seeds of 1 vanilla pod
- For lemon buttercream, add the finely grated zest of 2 lemons
- For orange buttercream, add the finely grated zest of 2 oranges

EQUIPMENT

ELECTRIC MIXER WITH PADDLE ATTACHMENT

1 Place the butter, icing sugar, salt and your choice of flavouring into the bowl of an electric mixer and, using the paddle attachment, bring the mixture together on low speed. Then turn the speed up and beat the buttercream until light and fluffy.

2 If not using it immediately, store in a sealed container in the fridge and bring it back to room temperature before use. Buttercream has a shelf life of up to 2 weeks if refrigerated.

Belgian Chocolate Ganache

MAKES 600G – roughly the amount you will need to layer a 20cm (8-inch) cake tier.

300g dark couverture chocolate drops (minimum 53% cocoa content)
300ml single cream

For other sizes and quantities please refer to the guide on page 143.

EQUIPMENT

HEATPROOF MIXING BOWL
SAUCEPAN
WHISK

1 Place the chocolate in a bowl and melt in a microwave cooker or over a bain-marie.

2 Place the cream in a saucepan, stir well and heat it up to a bare simmer.

3 Pour the hot cream over the chocolate (see 1) and whisk together (see 2). Don't over-whisk the ganache, as it splits easily.

4 Cool slightly until just hardening (see 3) before use. It can be stored in a sealed container in the fridge for up to a month.

Layering and Icing Cakes

Tiered wedding cakes, and also miniature cakes, provide the option of mixing different flavours of cake. If you would like to make a tiered wedding cake with different flavours, you must bear in mind that the bottom tier has to carry the weight of the other tiers and therefore a stronger cake base needs to be used for the bottom tiers and lighter cakes for the top. For example, if you are following my recipes, I recommend using chocolate cake for the lower tiers and the lighter Victoria sponge-based cakes for the upper tiers.

You will find a full portion guide and charts indicating amounts of basic cake mixtures, fillings and covering required for various types and sizes of cakes on page 143. A template for the positioning of dowels to support cake tiers is also given on the inside back cover.

Miniature Cakes

I usually bake and layer miniature cakes 3 days in advance, ice them on the next day and add the decoration 1 day before the event.

MAKES 24 ROUND MINIATURE CAKES

30cm (12-inch) square Victoria sponge cake
(see page 122)

For the filling:

about 3 tablespoons jam, marmalade, lemon curd or chocolate ganache (see page 126)

small amount of icing sugar for dusting

about 500g buttercream or ganache
(see pages 125–6), flavoured to your choice

2kg marzipan

2kg sugar paste

small amount of clear alcohol (I use vodka as it has a neutral taste) or water

EQUIPMENT

LARGE BREAD KNIFE

LARGE PALETTE KNIFE

TRAY OR PLATE

CLING FILM

SMALL PALETTE KNIFE

SMALL PAN

LARGE ROLLING PIN

5CM (2-INCH) ROUND HIGH (5CM/2-INCH) PASTRY CUTTER OR MOUSSE RING

GREASEPROOF PAPER

5MM (¼ INCH) GUIDE STICKS

SMALL KITCHEN KNIFE

2 CAKE SMOOTHERS

25 X 5CM (2-INCH) ROUND CAKE CARDS (OPTIONAL)

1 Using a bread knife, trim the top crust off your sponge, then cut it horizontally into two even squares.

2 Using a large palette knife, spread one of the sponge halves with a thin layer of your chosen filling and then place the other one on top of that. Sandwiched together, the cake should be just less than about 5cm (2 inches) high.

3 Place the sponge cake on top of a tray or plate and wrap it thoroughly with cling film.

4 Chill the wrapped filled sponge for at least a couple of hours until it feels nice and firm.

5 Once the sponge is cold and firm, cut out 25 miniature cakes using the round, high 5cm (2-inch) pastry cutter and place them on a tray lined with cling film or greaseproof paper.

6 Using a small palette knife, carefully coat the sides and top of each of the cakes with either buttercream or ganache. Place each of the coated cakes on a little round cake card, using a tiny dab of buttercream or ganache to stick them in place. Return the cakes to the fridge and chill them until the coating is set.

7 Once the coating is firmly set, on a smooth surface lightly dusted with icing sugar, knead one-quarter of the marzipan until smooth and pliable. Shape it into a ball and then, using the rolling pin and the guide sticks, roll it out to a square of about 20cm (8 inches) and 5mm (¼-inch) thick.

8 Take 4 cakes out of the fridge. Cut the marzipan square into 4 even pieces and lay each one centred over the top of each cake. Carefully push the marzipan down the sides so that it will stick to them. Trim the excess off, using a small kitchen knife.

9 Run the cake smoothers along the sides and the top of each cake until the sides are straight and the top is nice and level.

10 Once all the cakes are covered with marzipan, thinly brush the outsides with clear alcohol or water and repeat steps 6 to 9, using sugar paste instead of marzipan. Let dry completely before decoration, preferably overnight.

My Favourite Cake and Filling Combinations

• **Vanilla sponge**, infused with vanilla syrup, layered with raspberry preserve and vanilla buttercream

• **Lemon sponge**, infused with lemon and Limoncello syrup, layered with lemon curd and lemon buttercream

• **Orange sponge**, infused with orange and Grand Marnier syrup, layered with luxury orange marmalade and orange buttercream

• **Rich dark chocolate cake** layered with Belgian chocolate ganache and Bailey's cream liqueur

Large Cakes

For a 20cm (8 inch) round cake tier you will need two 22.5cm (9 inch) round sponges (see the quantities guide on page 143).

For a Victoria Sponge Cake:
about 600g buttercream
2 tablespoons jam, marmalade, or lemon curd

For a Rich Dark Chocolate Cake:
about 600g chocolate ganache
small amount of icing sugar for dusting
about 850g marzipan
small amount of clear alcohol
   (I use vodka as it has a neutral taste)
about 850g sugar paste

For other sizes and quantities please refer to the guides on page 143.

EQUIPMENT
LARGE BREAD AND SMALL KITCHEN KNIVES
20CM (8 INCH) ROUND CAKE BOARD
LARGE PALETTE KNIFE
METAL SIDE SCRAPER
LARGE ROLLING PIN
5MM (¼ INCH) GUIDE STICKS
GREASEPROOF PAPER
METAL PIN OR FINE SCRIBER NEEDLE (PME)
2 CAKE SMOOTHERS
PASTRY BRUSH

1 Using a bread knife, trim the top crust off both sponges. Using the cake board as a template, trim the sides of each sponge to the exact size of the cake board.

2 Stick the bottom layer with the golden crust facing down on top of the cake board with a blob of buttercream or ganache.

3 Using a palette knife, spread it generously with fillings of your choice and then place the other piece of sponge on top.

4 Coat the cake with the remaining buttercream or ganache, spreading it first over the top and then down the sides (see 1). Remove excess with a metal scraper for the sides and a large palette knife for the top (see 2).

5 Chill for at least 2 hours. This layer should be firmly set before applying the next.

6 Once it is set, spread with another layer of buttercream or ganache and continue until the sides are straight and the top is level. Chill again until set, ideally overnight.

7 Dust a working surface with icing sugar, place the marzipan on top and knead until smooth and pliable. Shape into a ball and roll out to an even round 5mm (¼ inch) thick and large enough to cover the top and sides, using the rolling pin and guide sticks.

8 Remove the cake from the fridge and place on a sheet of greaseproof paper. Spread it with a very thin coat of butter-cream or ganache and place the marzipan sheet over the top, using the rolling pin to lift it from the work surface (see 1).

9 Push it down the sides, making sure that there are no air pockets trapped underneath. Should any appear, prick them with the metal pin and flatten them while the marzipan is still soft. Trim excess marzipan off the sides using a kitchen knife (see 2).

10 Run the cake smoother over the top and along the sides of the cake until it looks straight and smooth (see 3). Use the palms of your hands to smooth the edge. Let set for 1 or 2 days at cool room temperature.

11 Once set, brush the marzipan layer with a thin coat of clear alcohol to stick on the sugar paste. The alcohol not only destroys any bacteria that may have built up while storing the cake, but also evaporates within minutes after its application and therefore creates a strong and hygienic glue between the marzipan and the sugar paste. Should you prefer not to use alcohol, you can use boiled cold water instead.

12 Repeat steps 8 to 11 using sugar paste instead of marzipan.

Tips:
• For tiered cakes, start the preparation about 5 to 6 days before the event. For example, if the wedding is on a Saturday, bake the sponges on the Monday before and layer them on the Tuesday. Cover the cakes with marzipan on Wednesday and let it set overnight, so that it has time to dry. On Thursday, cover the cakes with sugar paste and let it set again overnight. This gives you the whole of Friday to apply your decorations, which you can prepare a couple of weeks in advance.

• For single tiered cakes, start about 3 to 4 days before the event, as the cake can be covered with marzipan and sugar paste on the same day. To make 1 cake tier you need 2 sponges of the same size.

• For a well-proportioned tiered cake, each tier should ideally be about 8.5cm (3½ inches) high, including the cake board, before applying the marzipan and icing. Make sure that all tiers have the exact same height unless a mixture of different heights is intended.

Covering a Cake Board with Sugar Paste

Ice your cake board at least 1 or 2 days ahead, to ensure that the icing is well set before placing the cake on top.

icing sugar for dusting

small amount of clear alcohol or cold
   boiled water

sugar paste (see quantities guide on page 143)

EQUIPMENT

THICK CAKE BOARD OF THE REQUIRED SIZE

PASTRY BRUSH

ROLLING PIN

CAKE SMOOTHER

TURNTABLE

SMALL KITCHEN KNIFE

15MM WIDTH SATIN RIBBON TO COVER THE SIDES

METAL PIN, IDEALLY WITH A BEAD AT THE TOP

1 Dust the cake board thinly with icing sugar and brush it with a little alcohol or water (to make a glue for the sugar paste).

2 Roll the sugar paste out to about 3 mm (⅛ inch) thick and large enough to cover the cake board.

3 Using the rolling pin, lift the paste and lay it over the cake board (see 1).

4 Let the cake smoother glide carefully over the surface of the paste and push out any air bubbles.

5 Place the board on top of the turntable and push the paste down the sides with the cake smoother (see 2).

6 Trim the excess paste off with a knife (see 3) and let the sugar paste dry for 1 to 2 days.

7 Once the paste is dry, wind the ribbon around the edge of the board and fix the ends with a metal pin (see 4).

Assembling and Stacking Tiered Cakes

FOR A 3-TIER CAKE

iced cake board about 7.5-10cm (3-4 inches)
    larger then the bottom tier (here I used a
    35cm (14-inch) board
small amount of royal icing (see page 136)
3 iced cake tiers of different sizes, e.g.
    25cm (10 inches), 17.5cm (7 inches) and
    10cm (4 inches)

EQUIPMENT

8 PLASTIC DOWELS

PALETTE KNIFE

STRONG SCISSORS OR SERRATED KNIFE

FOOD COLOUR PEN

DOWEL TEMPLATE (SEE INSIDE BACK COVER)

15MM WIDTH SATIN RIBBON TO FIT THE CAKE
    BASES (IF REQUIRED) AND THE BOARD

METAL PIN

SMALL SPIRIT LEVEL (OPTIONAL)

1 Using a palette knife, spread the centre of the iced cake board with a thin layer of royal icing, making sure the area doesn't exceed the size of the bottom cake tier.

2 Carefully lift your bottom tier with the palette knife and place it centred on top of the cake board (see 1).

3 Using the dowel template as a guide, mark the correct positions for the dowels on your cake and push 4 cake dowels vertically down the bottom cake (see 2). Cake dowels are used to stop the upper tiers from sinking into the lower tiers.

4 Mark each dowel about 1mm above the point where it exits the cake with a food colour pen.

5 Carefully remove the dowels, line them up next to each other and saw or cut them to the same length using the average mark as a guide line. Then stick them back into the cake. To check if all the dowels have the same height, place a cake board, if at hand, on top of the dowels and check that it sits straight, ideally using a small spirit level. Should you have to readjust the length of a dowel, carefully pull it out with the help of a pair of tweezers.

6 Once happy with the length and positioning of your dowels, spread a small amount of icing into the middle of the cake, carefully lift the second tier with a palette knife and centre it on top of the bottom tier.

7 Repeat steps 3–5 for the other tiers.

8 Measure the circumference of each tier and the cake board and cut a piece of ribbon about 1 cm (½ inch) longer than required in each case. Place the ribbon around the base of each tier and fix the ends with a small dab of icing. Use the metal pin to fix the ribbon around the cake board. Make sure all joins are at the back of the cake.

8 To cover the joins between tiers, pipe a thin line of icing along the bottom edge of each tier and, while it is still wet, run a finger over that to smooth it out (see 3).

Tip: depending on the transport and distance to the event, it may be safer to assemble a tiered wedding cake on site. You can dowel the cakes and fix the ribbons in advance and carry the tiers individually in separate boxes.

Dipping Cup Cakes and Fondant Fancies

Liquid fondant is widely used as a filling for chocolate truffles, etc., or as a glaze for pastries. It has a very long shelf life and tastes deliciously smooth when flavoured with fruit juices, essences or liqueurs. As it is white, it provides an ideal base for mixing brilliant colours.

Made by boiling together sugar, glucose syrup and water, it requires experience and skill to achieve the right consistency. To keep it simple, I use ready-made fondant.

MAKES ABOUT 25

20cm (8-inch) square Victoria sponge
  (see page 122), well soaked with syrup
  (see page 125) and layered with the filling
  of your choice (see pages 125–6)
1 heaped tablespoon sieved apricot jam
icing sugar for dusting
about 150g marzipan
1kg ready-made fondant from Almond Art
  (or use the powdered version from Squires
Kitchen and make up as per instructions)
small amount of liquid glucose
selection of liquid food colours
small amount of fruit juice, essence or liqueur

EQUIPMENT

BREAD KNIFE

TRAY

CLING FILM

PASTRY BRUSH

LARGE ROLLING PIN

SMALL KNIFE

MICROWAVE COOKER

SMALL BOWLS

TRUFFLE FORK

WIRE COOLING RACK

ROUND SILVER PAPER CASES (THEY DON'T MAKE
  SQUARE ONES, BUT THESE MOULD TO SHAPE)

1 Using a bread knife, trim off the dark top layer from your sponge. Turn the sponge upside down on the tray. It should have an even height of about 3–4 cm (1¼–1½ inches).

2 Wrap in cling film and chill for 2–3 hours.

3 Once the sponge is cool and firm, warm the apricot jam, unwrap the sponge and spread a thin layer of jam over the top, using the pastry brush.

4 On a work surface lightly dusted with icing sugar, knead the marzipan until smooth and pliable. Shape it to a ball and roll it out to a square large enough to cover the top of the sponge and about 3mm thick.

5 Carefully lift it and lay it over the top of the cake (see 1). Trim the excess, if necessary.

6 Slice the marzipan-topped sponge into 4cm (1½ inch) squares (see 2) and brush the tops with a thin layer of apricot jam.

7 Put the fondant in a large microwavable bowl and gently heat it in the microwave cooker at medium heat for about 1 minute. Stir in the glucose and heat again for about 20 seconds at a time, until it is warm and runny. (Alternatively, heat it in a saucepan over very low heat, stirring. Do not allow the fondant to boil, or it will lose its shine.) If necessary, add a little water or sugar syrup to make it more liquid (you are looking for a thick pouring consistency).

8 If you would like to mix the fondant with different colours, divide it between some plastic bowls and add a few drops of food colour at a time until you achieve the desired shades. Flavour the fondant to taste.

9 Dip one cake at a time upside down into the fondant, until about three-quarters of the sides are covered. To lift out, hold with one finger at the bottom and a truffle fork at the top (see 3), ensuring you don't push the fork into the marzipan as it would tear it off. Quickly shake off the excess fondant icing and place the cake on to the cooling rack, then leave it for the icing to set.

10 Carefully remove the fancies from the rack by cutting them loose at the bottom using a small kitchen knife and place in the paper cases. This is best done with slightly wet fingers, to prevent the icing sticking to them. Gently push the sides of the paper case against the sides of the cake and, as they stick, they take on the square shape. Place the cakes closely next to each other until ready for decoration. Again, this will help the paper cases stay square.

11 Iced fondant fancies keep for about 7 days in a cake box or wrapped in foil. Don't store them in the fridge or the icing will dissolve.

Cup Cakes

MAKES 20

2 heaped tablespoons sieved apricot jam
20 cup cakes (see Victoria Sponge, page 122),
    well soaked with sugar syrup (see page 125)
1kg pot of ready-made liquid fondant
small amount of liquid glucose
small amount of fruit juice, essence or liqueur
selection of food colours

EQUIPMENT

PASTRY BRUSH

MICROWAVE COOKER

SMALL BOWLS

SMALL PALETTE KNIFE OR SPOON

1 Warm the apricot jam and brush a thin layer over the top of each cup cake to seal it.

2 Put the fondant in a large microwavable bowl and gently heat in the microwave cooker at medium heat for 1 minute. Stir in the glucose and heat again for 20 seconds at a time, until warm and runny. (Or, heat in a saucepan over very low heat, stirring. Do not allow the fondant to boil, or it will lose its shine.) If necessary, add a little water or sugar syrup to make it more liquid (you are looking for a thick pouring consistency).

3 If you would like to mix the fondant with different colours, divide it between some plastic bowls and add a few drops of colour at a time until you get the desired shades.

4 Dip all the cup cakes of one colour first into the fondant, shake off excess and let set before moving on to the next colour. By the time you have dipped the last cup cakes, the icing of the first will have set and you can begin with the second coat of icing, as before. Dipping each cake twice will ensure a beautifully smooth and shiny surface.

5 Any leftover fondant icing can be stored in a bowl wrapped with cling film. Before using it again, pour some hot water over the top to soften the hardened top layer and leave it to soak for about 15 minutes, then pour off the water and heat as usual.

Tip: To save fondant and washing up, I start by mixing lighter fondant shades first and then add more fondant and food colour to the same bowl as required. Another way of working more economically is to mix different coloured icings to achieve a new colour. For example, to make yellow, blue and green icing, start with yellow in one bowl and blue in another. Then mix these together to make green icing.

Royal Icing and Basic Piping Techniques

Piping with royal icing is probably the one essential skill needed for most of my designs, particularly for decorating cookies. Made from icing sugar and either fresh egg white or dried powdered egg white, it also makes an excellent glue for fixing sugar flowers and other decorations on to cakes. Making royal icing is a very simple procedure; should you find it daunting, however, you can buy ready-made versions at specialist cake decorating suppliers.

Royal Icing

MAKES ABOUT 1KG

about 25g merriwhite (dried egg white
　　powder) or whites of 4 medium eggs
1kg icing sugar, sifted
squeeze of lemon juice

EQUIPMENT
SIEVE
ELECTRIC MIXER WITH PADDLE ATTACHMENT
SPOON
SEALABLE PLASTIC CONTAINER
J-CLOTH

▶**1** If using the merriwhite, mix with 150ml water and sieve to get rid of any lumps. Ideally let this rest overnight in the fridge.

▶**2** Place the sugar in the bowl of an electric mixer, add three-quarters of the merriwhite mix or the lightly beaten egg whites and the lemon juice, and start mixing on low speed.

▶**3** Once these are well combined, check the consistency. If the sides of the bowl still look dry and crumbly, add some more merriwhite or egg white until the icing looks almost smooth but not wet.

Stiff-peak consistency – for piping sugar flowers and leaves

Soft-peak consistency – for piping lines, dots and borders

Runny consistency – for filling in the centres of spaces

4 Keep mixing for about 4–5 minutes, until it has reached stiff-peak consistency.

5 Spoon into a sealable plastic container, cover with a clean damp j-cloth and the lid. Store at room temperature for up to 7 days; if using fresh egg, store in the refrigerator. The egg white can separate from the sugar after a couple of days, which will turn the icing into a dry, dense mixture. In such a case, remix at low speed until smooth and at stiff-peak consistency again. Make sure that no dried icing bits sticking to the sides of your storage container get into the mixing bowl.

Royal Icing Consistencies

Throughout the book, I will refer to the three useful consistencies of royal icing (as opposite), which are important in achieving the right results. Simply thin down your basic royal icing recipe with water, a little at a time, using a palette knife, until you have reached the right consistency. Always make sure you keep your icing covered with cling film or a damp cloth when not using it, to stop it from drying out.

Making a Paper Piping Bag

1 Take a square of greaseproof paper, about 35 x 35cm (14 x 14 inches), and fold one corner over to the opposite one. Cut the fold with a sharp knife (see 1).

2 Take one of the resulting paper triangles and hold it with your left hand at the middle of the longest side and with your right hand at the corner on the opposite (see 2).

3 Now move your right hand over to the right corner and curl it over to the top corner, so that it forms a cone (see 3).

4 Now move your left hand to the left corner and roll it around the cone until all corners meet at the top on the back of the cone.

5 Adjust the corners by moving them back and forth between your thumb and fingers until the cone forms a sharp point (see 4).

6 Fold the corners inside, tear at each side of the seam and fold the flap inside (see 5).

7 Only half fill and close by folding the side with the seam over to the plain side twice.

Basic Piping Techniques

First snip a small tip off your piping bag already filled with icing.

PIPING LINES

1 Hold the bag between the thumb and the fingers of your preferred hand and use the index finger of your other hand to guide the nozzle.

2 Touch the starting point with the tip of the bag and slowly squeeze out the icing. As you are squeezing, lift the bag slightly and pull the line straight towards you or, for example, along the sides of a cookie.

3 Once you are approaching the finishing point, gradually bring the bag down, stop squeezing and drop the line by touching the finishing point with the tip of the bag.

PIPING DOTS

1 Hold the tip of your piping bag 1mm above the surface and squeeze out the icing to produce a dot on the surface.

2 Gradually lift the tip as the dot gets larger.

3 Once the dot has reached its desired size, stop squeezing and lift off the tip.

4 Should the dot form a little peak at the top, flatten it carefully with a damp soft artist's brush.

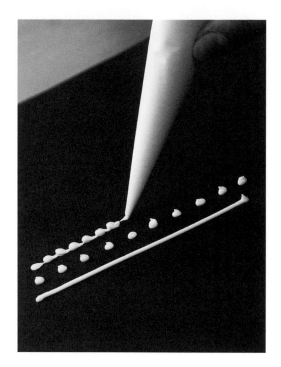

PIPING DOTTED BORDERS

1 Start as you would for piping a dot.

2 Once the dot has reached the required size, stop squeezing and pull the tip of your bag down, stopping where the next dot should start.

3 Repeat the process, making sure the dots are all the same size and equidistant. After a while, you will notice that you get into a flowing motion and your border looks nice and even.

Making Sugar Roses

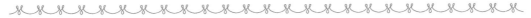

Making roses from sugar flower paste is a traditional craft that has always fascinated me. It takes time and skill making this type of rose, as each petal is shaped and stuck on individually, but I find the result very rewarding, as its fine delicate petals look almost natural, which makes it an ideal decoration for a sophisticated wedding cake. The exact amount of sugar flower paste required does, of course, depend on the size of the roses you make.

FOR ABOUT 5 MEDIUM-SIZED OPEN ROSES

250g sugar flower paste
small amount of white vegetable fat
selection of edible paste colours
cornflour for dusting
edible glue
selection of blossom tint dusting colours

EQUIPMENT

ROSE PETAL CUTTER SET (ORCHARD R1-4)
CALYX CUTTERS IN DIFFERENT SIZES
ROSE LEAF CUTTERS IN DIFFERENT SIZES
ROSE LEAF VEINING MAT
BONE TOOL
SMALL NON-STICK PLASTIC BOARD
STAY FRESH MULTI MAT
SMALL ROLLING PIN
FLOWER FOAM PAD
ABOUT 10 TEASPOONS AND 10 TABLESPOONS
WOODEN TOOTHPICKS
BLOCK OF POLYSTYRENE OR CAKE DUMMY
SELECTION OF SMALL ARTIST'S BRUSHES
SMALL SAUCEPAN
SEALABLE PLASTIC BAGS OR CLING FILM

For a rosebud you need 1 centre cone and 3 petals (see 1–3)

For a half-open rose you need 1 centre cone and 6 petals (see 4)

For an open rose you need 1 centre cone and 11 petals (see 5)

For a wide-open rose you need 1 centre cone and 18 petals (see 6)

The size of roses you need depends on the size of cake they will be used for.

For my Romantic Rose Cake on page 110 and Homage to Cath Kidston cake on page 104, I used cutters R1 (about 4.5cm long) and R2 (about 3.5cm long), but if you have a different rose cutter set it will do just as well.

Make the rose centres at least a day ahead.

1 Knead the flower paste until smooth and pliable and add a small amount of the white vegetable fat if it feels hard and brittle.

2 Knead in the paste colour as required, a little at the time. If you want to make different colours of roses, divide the paste into portions and dye them first. Wrap in a sealable plastic bag and rest for about 30 minutes. Allow some extra for the green leaves.

3 To shape the rose centres take a small piece of flower paste and shape it to a cone that is slightly shorter than the petal cutter.

4 Apply a thin layer of vegetable fat to one end of a toothpick with your fingers. Then push the greased end vertically into the bottom of the cone. Stick the toothpick into

the styrofoam or cake dummy and let the cone dry for a couple of hours, ideally overnight. Prepare all the cones you need.

TO MAKE THE ROSEBUDS

▶5 To make the rose petals, place a piece of sugar flower paste on the plastic board dusted lightly with cornflour. Roll out until very thin, about 1mm. Stamp out petal shapes making sure edges are clean and sharp. Remove excess paste around the petals and wrap for later use. Cover the petals with the multi mat to stop them drying out.

▶6 Place petal no. 1 on to the foam pad. Keep the remaining petals covered.

▶7 Shape and stretch it by gently running the bone tool from the centre to the outside edge. Notice how the petal becomes slightly larger and the edge begins to frill.

▶8 Brush the surface of the petal thinly with edible glue, using a fine artist's brush.

▶9 Wrap tightly around the cone, round side up, making sure the tip is completely covered.

▶10 For the second row of rose petals, take another 2 petals from the plastic board and repeat steps 8 & 9.

▶11 Brush the bottom half of both petals thinly with the edible glue. Position the first of the 2 petals centred over the seam. Tuck the other slightly inside the previous petal and push the sides together. Slightly curve the edges out with your fingertips.

TO MAKE A HALF-OPEN ROSE:

▶12 Continue by laying another 3 petals of the same size around the rosebud, each one slightly overlapping. Again slightly curve the edges of the petals out with your fingertips.

TO MAKE AN OPEN ROSE

13 Before continuing with the next layer of petals make sure that the half-open rose is completely dry.

14 Shape another 5 petals that are a size larger than the previous one, as described in step 7, and lay each inside a spoon dusted with cornflower with the edges slightly overlapping the spoon. Curve the edges of the petals to the outside with your fingertips and them it dry for about 15 minutes, until they feel slightly rubbery. Letting the petals semi-dry inside a spoon gives them more volume and shape and they will look more realistic.

15 Brush the bottom half of both petals thinly with the edible glue and arrange them around the half-open rose as before. You may find that the petals are now a little bit too heavy to hold up while still wet. In this case turn the rose carefully upside down on to the polystyrene block or cake dummy and let dry.

TO MAKE A LARGE OPEN ROSE

16 Repeat step 13 to 15 using 7 petals.

DUSTING AND STEAMING SUGAR ROSES

17 Once all roses have completely dried, you can enhance and highlight their colour by dusting the edges of the petals with blossom tint colours of a complementary shade. For example, I have used plum for dusting the purple and pink roses on my Romantic Rose Cake on pages 110–113.

18 Dip a fine artist's brush into a small amount of colour powder and brush the edges of the petals with it from the outside towards the centre. You have to be very careful not to spill any colour as it is almost impossible to take it off. Shake off any excess powder.

19 Once you have dusted all your roses, boil some water in a small pan and hold each rose carefully over the steam for about 3 seconds. This will bring the colour to life and give the rose a satin-like sheen.

TO MAKE CALYXES AND LEAVES

20 Roll out some green flower paste to about 1mm thickness and stamp out the calyx and leaf shapes. Remove the excess paste and keep it covered for later use.

21 Place the calyx on to the foam pad and gently move the bone tool over its surface from the centre towards the edges to stretch and thin the edges slightly. Keep the leaves covered until later.

22 Brush a thin layer of edible glue over the top and stick it underneath the bottom of the rose. Pinch and shape the tips with your fingers as required.

23 Place the leaves on the foam pad and again gently stretch and thin the edges with the bone tool.

24 Press each leaf in the rose leaf veiner and shape slightly with your fingers for a natural look.

Tips:
Hand-crafted sugar roses can be made weeks or even months in advance as they have a very long shelf life. Make sure you protect them from dust and sunlight to keep the colour.

• Use a lighter colour shade for the centre of the rose and a darker one for the outside petals or vice versa. This will make your rose look even more natural.

• Some blossom tints are not edible, so check the label and remove the flowers from the cake before eating if you use those colours.

Glossary

Most items are available from specialist suppliers (below), although more everyday ones can be found in supermarkets and cookware shops.

INGREDIENTS

Fondant Made from sugar, water and cream of tartar, fondant is widely used as a glaze in confectionery as well as in pâtisserie and cake decorating. Ready-made fondant is available in a block or as a powder to be mixed with water.

Food colours The food colours used in this book are those in either liquid or paste form. The pastes are more concentrated than the liquids and therefore more useful for colouring sugar pastes and marzipans. Liquid colours mix faster and give more even results with royal icing.

Glitter, edible Make sure it is edible, not simply non-toxic.

Glucose, liquid A thick version of corn syrup used to make fondant icing in order to give it a beautiful shine.

Gum tragacanth Made from the dried sap of the Astragalus plant, this is sold as a powdered hardening agent and is mixed with sugar paste to create a pliable modelling paste for making sugar flowers. It has the further effect of making the paste set on contact with air. It may also be mixed with a little water to make an edible glue.

Lustre (or luster), edible This non-toxic pearl dust comes in different shades. It can either be mixed to a thick paste with a drop of alcohol or applied directly with an artist's brush.

Marzipan Made from ground almonds and icing sugar, marzipan is used for covering large cakes before icing, as it seals in moisture as well as helping to stabilize shape. It is also ideal for making flowers, as it is very easy to mould and the individual petals stick to each other naturally.

Merriwhite This is dried egg white powder used instead of fresh egg whites in making royal icing for food safety reasons, as the dried egg white is pasteurized.

Sugar flower paste or gum paste A fine and pliable paste made from icing sugar, gelatine and gum tragacanth, which dries hard, with a porcelain-like texture. It is used to make finely crafted sugar flowers.

Sugar paste A very smooth and pliable icing made from gelatin, icing sugar and water, which dries hard but is still easy to cut. Sugar paste is used for covering cakes and for making flowers and modelling cake decorations.

EQUIPMENT

Bone tool A long plastic stick with rounded ends, looking like a bone, this is used to shape sugar paste petals.

Cake smoothers These are flat rectangular pieces of smooth plastic, with a handle, used to smooth the marzipan and sugar paste on a cake.

Cel stick This is a thin plastic stick for shaping flowers.

Foam pad This is used as a yielding surface for thinning the edges of flower paste with a bone tool (above).

Flower cutters Made of metal or plastic, flower cutters are used to cut petals and leaves out of flower paste. In this book I have used cutters to make roses, petunias, primroses and violets.

Flower nail Used for making royal icing sugar flowers. It functions as a base for the piping, as it may be turned readily in the non-piping hand.

Guide sticks Long sticks used to roll out dough or sugar paste to an even thickness.

Leaf veiner/veining mat A rubber mat used for shaping and marking leaves made of flower paste or marzipan.

Rose and leaf embosser Usually made of plastic, embossers are used to push the impression of a pattern into icing.

Rose calyx cutter Used for cutting the calyx for a rose out of flower paste or marzipan.

Side scraper Flat piece of metal (ideally stainless steel) with a straight side used for scraping excess cream off the side of a cake when filling. It helps give perfectly straight sides.

Stay fresh multi mat Thick acetate mat used to cover rolled-out sugar (flower) paste to prevent drying out.

Suppliers

For general cake decorating tools and equipment:

UK

Jane Asher Party Cakes
24 Cale Street
London SW3 3QU
www.jane-asher.co.uk

Almond Art
Unit 15 & 16 Phoenix Road
Crowther Industrial Estate
Washington,
Tyne and Wear
NE38 0AD
www.almondart.com

Design A Cake
30–31 Faraday Close
Gorse Lane Industrial Estate
Clacton-on-Sea, Essex
CO15 4TR
www.design-a-cake.co.uk

Squires Shop and School
Squires House
3 Waverley Lane
Farnham, Surrey
GU9 8BB
www.squires-group.co.uk

For edible lustre and glitter sparkle:

EdAble Art
1 Stanhope Close
The Grange,
Spennymoor
Co Durham DL16 6LZ
tel 01388 816309

For Ribbons

VV Rouleaux
54 Sloane Square
London SW1W 8AX
www.vvrouleaux.com

WORLDWIDE

AUSTRALIA

CAKE DECO
Shop 7, Port Phillip Arcade
232 Flinders Street
Melbourne, Victoria
Australia
www.cakedeco.com.au

GERMANY

Tortissimo Backzubehör
Carl-Benz-Str. 6
35305 Grünberg
Deutschland
www.tortissimo.de

THE NETHERLANDS

De leukste Taarten Shop
Meeuwstraat 10
1546 LR Jisp, Holland
www.deleukstetaartenshop.nl

USA

Sugarcraft, Inc.
2715 Dixie Hwy.
Hamilton, Ohio 45015
www.sugarcraft.com

For cookie cutters

Kitchen Collectables, Inc.
8901 J. Street, Suite 2
Omaha NE 68127, USA
www.kitchengifts.com

CopperGifts.com
900 N. 32nd St
Parsons, KS 67357, USA
www.coppergifts.com

 For more information on Peggy Porschen's cookies and cakes, or to place an order, please visit her website **peggyporschen.com**

CAKE MIX QUANTITY AND PORTION GUIDE

This chart will give an overview of what size cake you need for your number of guests and the approximate quantity of cake mix needed for the different sizes of cake tins.

The basic cake recipes in this book are based on a 20cm (8 inch) cake tin or 20–24 cakes or 25 fondant fancies. Please bear in mind that for each cake tier you will need 2 sponges, i.e. double the amount of cake mix, baked in 2 tins of the same size (except for the Bed of Roses Cake on page 86). The figure shown in the second column below indicates by how much the basic recipe needs to be multiplied.

I also recommend baking a cake 2.5cm (1 inch) larger than required, as sponge shrinks during baking and the sides are usually a bit dry. After baking, trim the edges with a serrated knife down to the exact size required, using the cake board as a guide.

Cake Tin Size (round or square)	Multiply basic recipe by	Cake Portions 2.5x2.5cm (1x1 inch) round/square	Mini Cakes	Cup Cakes	Fondant Fancies
10cm (4 inch)	¼	10 / 16			
12.5cm (5 inch)	⅓	12 / 20			
15cm (6 inch)	½	20 / 35			
17.5cm (7 inch)	¾	25 / 45			
20cm (8 inch)	1	40 / 60	9	20-24	25
22.5cm (9 inch)	1⅓	50 / 80			
25cm (10 inch)	2	60 / 100	16	40-48	36
27.5cm (11 inch)	2½	80 / 120			
30cm (12 inch)	3¼	90 / 140	25		
35cm (14 inch)	4¼	130 / 185			

• If you want a large centrepiece, but only need a small amount of cake, use a fake tier in between real tiers. Tell the bride and groom, to avoid them trying to cut it.

Quantity guide for marzipan and sugar paste, and buttercream or chocolate ganache filling

The figures below give you the approximate amounts required for cakes of different sizes, round or square, with a height of 8.5cm (3½ inches).

CAKE / BOARD SIZE	MARZIPAN / SUGAR PASTE	SUGAR PASTE FOR CAKE BOARD	BUTTERCREAM / GANACHE
10cm (4 inch)	400g		150g (also 25 fondant fancies)
12.5cm (5 inch)	500g		225g
15cm (6 inch)	600g	300g	300g
17.5cm (7 inch)	750g	400g	450g (also 20–24 cup cakes)
20cm (8 inch)	850g	600g	600g (also 25 mini cakes)
22.5cm (9 inch)	1kg	700g	750g
25cm (10 inch)	1.25kg	800g	900g
27.5cm (11 inch)	1.5kg	850g	1.2kg
30cm (12 inch)	1.75kg	900g	1.5kg
32.5cm (13 inch)	2kg	950g	1.75kg
35cm (14 inch)	2.5kg	1kg	2kg

Acknowledgements

The success of my first book, *Pretty Party Cakes* was absolutely overwhelming. I would like to thank all the readers who have sent me the most wonderful encouraging letters and emails from all over the world and I hope that this book will live up to your expectations and inspire you just as much.

I would also like to thank Alison Cathie, Jane O'Shea and Helen Lewis of Quadrille Publishing for signing me up for another beautiful project and letting me explore my favourite subject area – making cakes and cookies for romantic occasions. As always, it has been an absolute joy working with all of you.

A big thank you to my dream team: Georgia Glynn Smith for your phenomenal photography; Lewis Esson, you are my wizard of words; and Chalkley Calderwood Pratt for your beautiful eye for design and layout. Once again it has been a privilege and an inspiration to work with all of you.

None of this would have been possible without the loving support, encouragement and inspiration of my partner Bryn, my parents Iris and Helmut, and my brother Tom. I am eternally grateful for everything you have done for me.

Last, but not least, I would like to thank my team at Peggy Porschen cakes and all our loyal clients for their support and trust that have made it possible for me to establish Peggy Porschen cakes as one of the UK's leading cake design companies.

Index